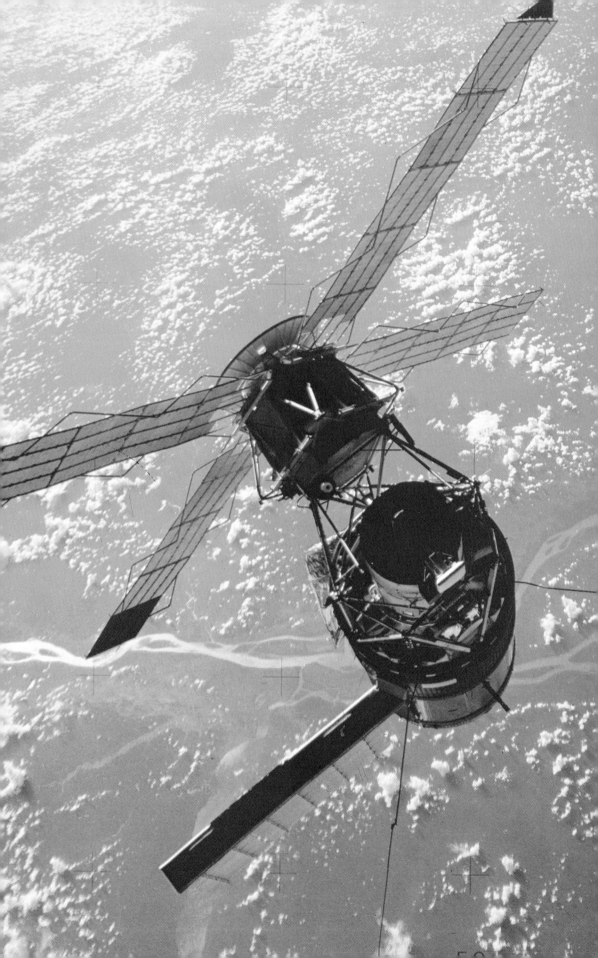

Young
People's
Science
Encyclopedia

YOUNG PEOPLE'S
SCIENCE ENCYCLOPEDIA

Edited by the Staff of
NATIONAL COLLEGE OF EDUCATION, Evanston, Illinois

ASSOCIATE EDITORS

HELEN J. CHALLAND, B.E., M.A., Ph.D.
   Chairman, Division of Natural Sciences
National College of Education,
Evanston, Illinois

DONALD A. BOYER, B.S., M.S., Ph.D.
   Science Education Consultant, Winnetka
Public Schools, Winnetka, Illinois
Science, National College of Education

EDITORIAL CONSULTANTS
ON THE STAFF OF NATIONAL COLLEGE OF EDUCATION

Elizabeth R. Brandt, B.A., M.Ed.
Eugene B. Cantelupe, B.A., M.F.A., Ph.D.
John H. Daugherty, B.S., M.A.
Irwin K. Feinstein, B.S., M.A., Ph.D.
Mary Gallagher, A.B., M.A., Ph.D.
Beatrice S. Garber, A.B., M.S., Ph.D.
Hal S. Galbreath, B.S. Ed., M.S.
Arthur J. Hannah, B.S., M.Ed., Ed.D.

Robert R. Kidder, A.B., M.A., Ph.D.
Jean C. Kraft, B.S., M.A., Ph.D.
Elise P. Lerman, B.A., B.F.A., M.F.A.
Mary M. Lindquist, B.A., M.A., Ph.D.
Mary-Louise Neumann, A.B., B.S.L.S.
Lavon Rasco, B.A., M.A., Ph.D.
Bruce Allen Thale, B.S.Ed., M.S.Ed.
Fred R. Wilkins, Jr., B.A., M.Ed., Ph.D.

SPECIAL SUBJECT AREA CONSULTANTS

Krafft A. Ehricke, B.A.E., H.L.D.
Benjamin M. Hair, A.B., M.D.
Charles B. Johnson, B.S., M.A., M.S.
Raymond J. Johnson, B.B.A., M.Ed.

H. Kenneth Scatliff, M.D.
Eleanor S. Segal, M.D.
Paul P. Sipiera, B.A., M.S.
Ray C. Soliday, B.A., B.S., M.A. (Deceased)

Don Dwiggins, Aviation Editor

THE STAFF

Project Director   Rudolph A. Hastedt
Project Editor   M. Frances Dyra
Senior Editor   Jim Hargrove
Editorial Assistant Janet Zelasko

Young People's
SCIENCE
Encyclopedia

Edited by the Staff of

NATIONAL COLLEGE OF EDUCATION

Evanston, Illinois

Volume 6/Di-Em

 CHILDRENS PRESS, CHICAGO

Photographs

Page 2:   Skylab space station (NASA)

Page 3:   *Top to Bottom:*
          Wheatfield (U.S.D.A. Photo)
          Technician capping Abbokinase (Abbott Laboratories)
          Spider (Macmillan Science Company)
          View of Earth (NASA)
          Space Shuttle (NASA)
          Bahama coral reef (Macmillan Science Company)

Cover: Designed by Sandy Gelak
         Sleeping Bear Dunes, Michigan (James P. Rowan)
         Red Rocket Electric Streetcar (James P. Rowan)
         Golden Eagle (Tom Smylie: U.S. Fish & Wildlife Service)

Library of Congress Catalog Card Number: 67-17925

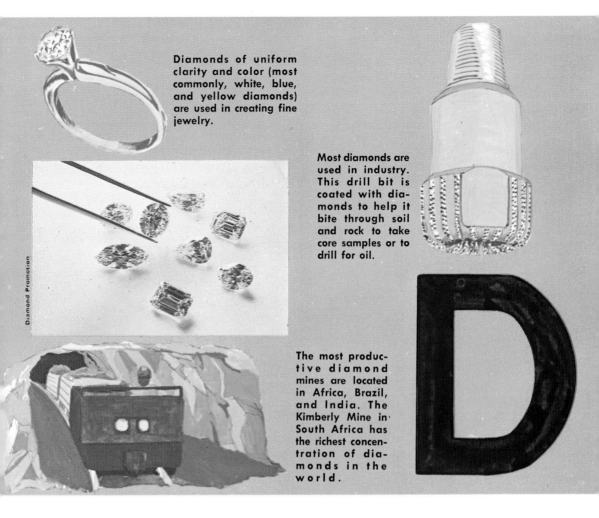

Diamonds of uniform clarity and color (most commonly, white, blue, and yellow diamonds) are used in creating fine jewelry.

Most diamonds are used in industry. This drill bit is coated with diamonds to help it bite through soil and rock to take core samples or to drill for oil.

The most productive diamond mines are located in Africa, Brazil, and India. The Kimberly Mine in South Africa has the richest concentration of diamonds in the world.

Diamond Promotion

Diamond Diamonds are one of the most precious gems. Diamonds are mined in deposits of gravel. Rough diamonds look like pebbles. They were formed from the element CARBON under great heat and pressure. A diamond is the hardest mineral known, yet the same chemical element makes coal, charcoal and graphite.

Like gold mining, diamond mining was once considered a romantic enterprise. Early mining methods gave the adventurous person excitement. If he came upon a rich find, his fortune was assured. However, nowadays the search for diamonds is only one phase of a highly-organized industry in which machines play an important part.

The diamond is a natural, crystallized form of carbon. It is the only gem stone that is composed of a single element. It has perfect cleavage. That means that if the stone is fractured by a sharp blow in a cleavage direction, it comes apart smoothly.

A diamond refracts and breaks light up into the different colors of the SPECTRUM. This property, as well as clarity and transparency, gives it an unsurpassed brilliance. No chemical can affect it, but temperatures of 900° C. (1652° F.) can damage it.

Since the diamond is the hardest substance known to man, it is used for cutting, grinding, or boring into hard metals and other hard substances. Sometimes whole diamonds are used for industrial purposes, while in other cases they are first crushed and cemented into a desired shape. Diamonds make the best wire-drawing dies. A tapered hole is cut through the diamond, and the metal is drawn through this hole. As expected, diamonds can be cut only by other diamonds.

Recently, a crude grade of synthetic diamond has been made in special high-pressure machines. These are industrial grade diamonds. Industrial diamonds serve as watch BEARINGS and as cutting tools.

V. V. N.

SEE ALSO: CRYSTAL, GEM

507

Diaphragm (DYE-uh-framm) In anatomy, the diaphragm is a partition of tendons and muscles which separates the thoracic or chest cavity from the abdominal cavity in mammals. In other areas of science, a diaphragm is a thin partition or membrane.

SEE: RESPIRATORY SYSTEM

Diarrhea (dye-uh-REE-uh) Diarrhea is a condition in which there are frequent, watery bowel movements. It is a symptom of many diseases. One must determine what has caused the condition. It is often but a short-lasting ailment. In such cases it is due to an effort of nature to rid the body of poisonous substances or indigestible food.

Some of the causes of diarrhea are the use of spoiled food stuffs and the use of food to which the individual is sensitive, as in an allergy. Diarrhea may be of nervous origin, the result of anxiety or fear. Unwise food combinations may have been indulged in or excesses of fats, rich food or candy.   H. K. S.

Diastole (dye-ASS-tuh-lee) The diastole is the normal, rhythmical relaxation, or *dilatation,* of the HEART muscle. During this stage, the chambers of the heart fill with BLOOD.

SEE: BLOOD PRESSURE

Diatom These tiny one-celled plants live in fresh water, salt water, and damp soil. Diatoms are golden brown ALGAE. Their hard cell walls form a minute round box with an overlapping cover.

Diatoms are tiny, 1-celled plants.

National Teaching Aids

Diatoms are one-celled but they may clump together to form colonies. They are classified in the *Chrysophyta* group with the yellow-green and golden-brown algae. There are about 16,000 species. They contain chlorophyll but this green coloring is hidden by the brown pigment. The cell is composed of two halves which overlap. The wall of *pectin* contains silica which does not decay after the plant dies. Food is stored, for the most part, as oil or fat instead of starch. Diatoms are found around soil deposits.

Diatomite, or *diatomaceous earth,* is used in filters for sugar refining, in insulation of blast furnaces, and as a polishing powder. It is also used in the manufacture of FERTILIZERS and high explosives such as dynamite.   J. M. C.

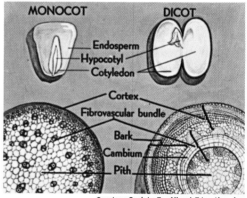

Courtesy Society For Visual Education, Inc.

A dicot differs from a monocot in more ways than the number of seed leaves. The tissue arrangement in the stems also varies

Dicotyledon (dye-caht-uh-LEE-duhn) Flowering plants are divided into two groups, monocotyledons and dicotyledons. Dicotyledons are those plants which have two seed leaves within the seed, like two halves in a pea.

Usually dicotyledons, or *dicots,* have their flower parts in groups of four or five—for example, five petals or ten stamens. The veins of a dicot's leaf grow in a network that starts at the base of the leaf and spreads throughout it to the edges. The conducting tissue in the stem of a dicot is arranged in concentric circles. These are the ANNUAL RINGS of a tree. About three quarters of all flowering plants belong in angiosperm subclass *Dicotyledonae.*
   J. M. C.

SEE ALSO: COTYLEDON, MONOCOTYLEDON

Didymium see Neodymium

Dieffenbachia (dee-fen-BAH-kee-uh) Dieffenbachia is a tropical, upright, shrubby, evergreen plant. Its handsome leaves may be spotted or feathered with white, cream, or yellow markings. The largest leaves may be 2 feet (.61 meter) long and 1 foot (.3 meter) wide. It belongs to the arum family.

Dielectric see Condenser

Dies Dies are carved metal blocks or plates, mounted in presses for the purpose of cutting out, shaping or engraving. The various kinds of dies include engraved stamps for making designs on metals as in coining money, steel plates with holes through which metal is drawn out into wire, and engraved plates for stamping designs or letters on paper and leather.
SEE: METAL

Diesel see Engine

Differential When an AUTOMOBILE rounds a corner, the outside wheels must travel faster than the inside wheels to prevent skidding. At the same time, both inside and outside wheels must be driven by the same source of power. The differential is an arrangement of gears which makes this possible.

Diffraction Diffraction is the bending of LIGHT, SOUND, or electromagnetic waves which results when an object interferes with the normal course or strength of the waves.
SEE: ELECTROMAGNETIC SPECTRUM

Diffraction grating A diffraction grating is a device now used to break light into a rainbow in most spectral instruments instead of a prism.

There are two types of diffraction gratings: reflection gratings and transmission gratings. A grating has a series of parallel lines on it. The lines are close together. The number of lines varies from 400 to 6,000 per centimeter. When light passes through the spaces of a transmission grating, thin rays are formed. The rays spread out and come together. When the rays come together a SPECTRUM is formed.   A.J.H.

Diffusion Diffusion is the penetration of the molecules of one substance into another. Liquids, gases and solids diffuse. It is caused by the constant motion of the molecules. When it takes place within an enclosure, it results in uniform concentration.
SEE: GAS, MOLECULE, OSMOSIS, PHYSICAL STATES AND CHANGES

✳ **THINGS TO DO**

PROVING THAT MOLECULES OF LIQUIDS ARE IN CONSTANT MOTION

1 Place several glasses of water on a table where they remain for two days without being moved.
2 Put a cube of sugar in one, a piece of rock salt in another, a tablet of vegetable dye in a third, and a piece of hard candy in the last. Do not stir the liquids.
3 What happens to each material?
4 Taste the two glasses containing the sugar and salt. What color is the water in the other glasses?
5 Molecules of liquids and gases are constantly moving around. Any solid which will dissolve in a liquid is soon spread by diffusion.

✳ **THINGS TO DO**

WHAT CAN YOU LEARN ABOUT DIGESTION?
WHAT REACTION DOES SALIVA HAVE ON CERTAIN FOODS?

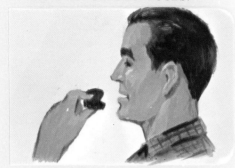

1 Start to chew a cracker or piece of bread. What does it taste like?
2 Continue to chew it for several minutes. Has the taste of it changed?
3 The enzyme amylase in saliva has started to change starch to sugar.

Digestive system The work of the digestive system in an animal is to break food into substances small enough for the cells to use. This system is made up of two kinds of organs. Some organs are hollow, and the food travels through them. They make up the *digestive tract*. Other organs are solid and never touch the food. These organs, called *digestive glands,* make some of the juices which break up food. The juices made in these glands are called *enzymes*.

Every animal must digest food before it can use it for ENERGY or growth and repair. One-celled animals and sponges have no digestive systems. They digest food inside a bubble, called a *vacuole*. The vacuole forms temporarily inside the cell. The simplest animals with digestive systems are the COELENTERATA such as hydra. They have a mouth and a sac-like structure in the center of their bodies. The EARTHWORM has more organs than

these water animals. A lower animal has an opening at the end of the digestive tract for undigested food to pass out.

PARTS OF THE DIGESTIVE SYSTEM

The parts of the digestive systems of all animals are named for the kind of work they do. The *mouth* takes in and usually chops up the food. The SALIVARY GLANDS, found in most land animals, empty their secretions into the mouth and begin the process of digestion. The *pharynx*—the back of the mouth—receives the food next and passes it to the tube-like *esophagus*. Then the sac-like *stomach* receives the food. The stomach in many animals is used only for storage. In others, digestive glands are present in the lining, and digestion occurs there. Crayfish, BIRDS, and many plant-eating animals have stomachs with compartments or divisions for storage, extra grinding, and digestion. The *intestine* is the organ in which most digestion occurs. It usually has two parts, the narrow small intestine and the wider large intestine, or *colon*. The small intestine always has glands in its lining. Whenever two glands outside the tract, the LIVER and the PANCREAS, are present, they pour their secretions into the intestine. The surface of the intestine usually is increased by folds or a spiral valve so that food passes through it more slowly and so there is more digestive surface available. This enables more of the food to be absorbed by the CIRCULATORY SYSTEM. The end of the digestive tract through which the undigested food leaves the body is called the *anus*.

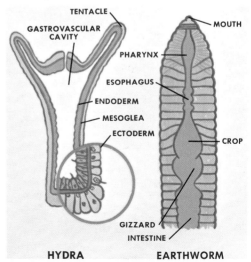

HYDRA   EARTHWORM

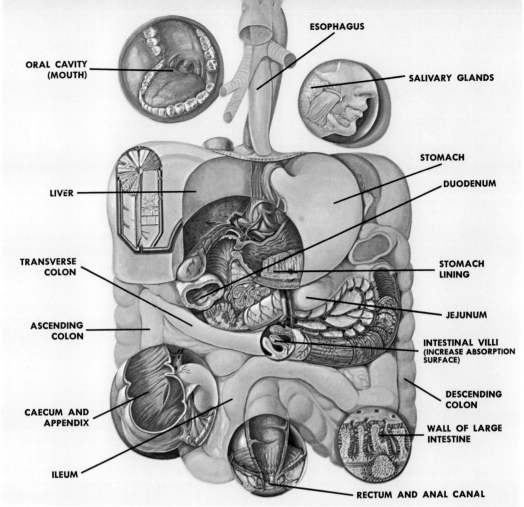

ORAL CAVITY (MOUTH)

ESOPHAGUS

SALIVARY GLANDS

LIVER

STOMACH

DUODENUM

TRANSVERSE COLON

STOMACH LINING

ASCENDING COLON

JEJUNUM

INTESTINAL VILLI (INCREASE ABSORPTION SURFACE)

DESCENDING COLON

CAECUM AND APPENDIX

WALL OF LARGE INTESTINE

ILEUM

RECTUM AND ANAL CANAL

©Denoyer-Geppert Co.

DIGESTION IN MAN

Man's digestive system has been well-studied by scientists. The human digestive tract begins with the mouth. The lips help push the food inside, and the tongue pushes the food between the teeth. Three pairs of salivary glands, two located at the joints of the jaws and one under the tongue, pour saliva, containing a digestive ENZYME, into the mouth through tiny tubes. Chewing not only breaks the food into smaller pieces but also mixes the food with saliva. The *mucous glands* of the mouth lubricate the food for easy swallowing. The pharynx in back of the *soft palate* enlarges to receive the food and pass it on to the 9-inch (22.86-centimeter) tube, the *esophagus,* which also contains mucous glands. The food is pushed down the esophagus by ring-like muscles which contract one after another. These waves of contractions, found throughout the digestive tract, are called *peristalsis.* The esophagus and stomach are connected at the *cardiac valve.* This is a strong ring of muscle which prevents the food from leaving the cardiac part of the stomach. At the lower end of the stomach is a similar valve called the *pyloric sphincter.* The stomach can hold about 2½ quarts (2.37 liters) of food. It acts as a reservoir and allows only a little food to enter the small intestine at one time. Gastric juice is made by about 35 million tiny glands in the stomach lining. In order for this juice to act on all the food, the stomach squeezes the food back and forth, breaking it into a thick liquid called *chyme.* The stomach empties completely in about 2½ hours.

The *small intestine* is a 23-foot (7-meter) tube about 1 inch (2.54 centimeters) in diameter. The first foot of the tube is called the *duodenum.* The liver, pancreas, and many tiny glands in the intestinal wall pour their secretions into the food here. The next 8 feet (2.44 meters) are the *jejunum,* and the last 14 feet (4.27 meters), the *ileum.* Most digestion and absorption occurs in the small intestine which has a very wrinkled surface. All over these folds are finger-like projections called *villi.* The villi contain tiny blood vessels and lymph vessels which absorb the digested food. The small intestine is long

511

✳ **THINGS TO DO**

**DOES PERISTALSIS WORK
AGAINST GRAVITY?**

1   **Stand on your head, balancing yourself against a wall. Take a bite of an apple, chew it well, then carefully swallow it.**
2   **Do you think it went to your stomach?**
3   **The muscles in your esophagus contract and expand pushing the food along regardless of the position of the body.**

and rough-surfaced. The liquid digested food passes through in about 3 hours.

The point at which the large and small intestines join is easily identified. Just as the wider large intestine begins, there is a pocket-like bulge with a worm-like object hanging from it. The pocket is the *cecum* and the "worm" is the APPENDIX. Neither has any use, and the appendix can be most harmful if food containing disease bacteria lodges in it. The large intestine is about 5 feet (1.52 meters) long and 2½ inches (6.35 centimeters) wide. The first 4½ feet (1.37 meters) are called the *colon,* the next 5 inches (12.7 centimeters), the *rectum,* and the last 1½ inches (3.81 centimeters), the *anal canal.* The waste material remains in the large intestine for 24 to 48 hours before leaving through the anus.

The food which all animals take in is of three kinds: CARBOHYDRATES (starches and sugars), PROTEINS, and FATS. The cells cannot use this food until it is broken down into water-soluble materials. The carbohydrates must become simple SUGARS—glucose, fructose, or galactose. The proteins must become AMINO ACIDS, and the fats, fatty acids, and glycerol. This breakdown is accomplished by the enzymes. Although the enzymes are unchanged at the end of digestion, they temporarily combine and react chemically with the food molecules.

CARBOHYDRATE DIGESTION

In man, carbohydrates are first attacked by AMYLASE, which is the enzyme in saliva. If the food is well chewed, the STARCH will be broken down into maltose. This is still too complex a sugar to be absorbed. The amylase cannot act in the stomach because HYDROCHLORIC ACID is present. When the carbohydrates reach the intestine, they are again attacked by many enzymes. The pancreatic juice contains *amylase* which acts on the starch not broken down by salivary amylase, changing it into maltose. The intestinal juice contains three enzymes which complete the sugar digestion. *Maltase* breaks maltose into glucose; *lactase* breaks lactose (milk sugar) into glucose and galactose; *sucrase* (invertase) separates sucrose (table sugar) into glucose and fructose. These sugars can now be absorbed into the blood by the capillaries of the villi.

PROTEIN DIGESTION

Protein digestion begins in the stomach. There *pepsin* is produced in the gastric glands and activated by hydrochloric acid. Pepsin breaks protein into less complex compounds called *peptones* and *proteoses.* Another enzyme, renin, is secreted only in babies and young children. It works on the casein protein in milk, causing the milk to curdle. Renin is not produced in adults. One of the enzymes secreted by the pancreas is *trypsinogen.* An enzyme in the intestine coverts it to *trypsin.* It breaks down proteins in the small intestine after they have left the stomach. The end products of protein digestion are amino acids. They pass through the villi into the capillaries and directly to the liver. The liver can easily change amino acids into glucose for ready energy.

FAT DIGESTION

Fats are not acted on until they reach the small intestine where they are mixed with *bile.* Bile is not an enzyme but is most essential to fat digestion. It is produced in the LIVER and stored temporarily in the sac-like *gall bladder.* When the small intestine receives food, it signals the gall bladder to contract. The bile is then forced into the intestine, and *emulsifies,* or makes tiny droplets of, the fat. Bile also contains salts necessary for absorption of glycerol and fatty acids. *Lipase,* produced by the pancreas, is the enzyme which acts on fats, and changes them to fatty acids and glycerol. These products do not enter the blood stream directly, but are absorbed through the lymph vessels *(lacteals)* of the villi.

VITAMINS and minerals need no digestion. The minerals are made soluble by the hydrochloric acid of the stomach. Vitamins B and C are water-soluble. Vitamins A, D, E, and K are oil-soluble and in the presence of bile salts can be absorbed.

Bile and hydrochloric acid also serve the digestive system by killing bacteria. Many bacteria enter with the food that is eaten. They would cause infection and food spoilage without the antiseptic action of these fluids.

Water, one of the necessities of all living things, is absorbed in small quantities throughout the digestive tract. Most water is absorbed in the colon. The chyme coming from the small intestine is liquid when it enters the colon. By the time it leaves the body, it is a semi-solid. Thus, the digestive system furnishes man with two basic necessities, food and water.   J.K.L.

SEE ALSO: EXCRETORY SYSTEM, PORIFERA, PROTOZOA

Digital computer see Computer

Digitalis
Digitalis is the name of a drug and the herb from which it is taken. It is the common FOXGLOVE of the figwort family which is native to southern Europe.

A flower stalk grows up from a rosette of coarse, alternate leaves. The white or purple blooms look like bells or tubes and are 2-3 inches (5.08-7.62 centimeters) long. It may be a biennial or perennial and flowers in early summer.

Digitonin, a dark green compound, is extracted from the dried leaves. It is used as a stimulant when the human heart fails. It produces stronger contractions and evens up the rhythm of the beats.   H.J.C.

SEE ALSO: PHARMACOLOGY

Dill

Dill
Dill is a favorite herb which dates back to Biblical times. The Greeks and Romans made wreaths of dill flowers for their conquering heroes. Dill grows wild in Europe, Africa, and southern Asia, but it is cultivated in North America.

The sturdy dill plant grows to 3 feet (.91 meters) and is shaped like an umbrella, with long wisps of bluish-green leaves and clusters of tiny yellow flowers.

The tender, young HERB is used for seasoning cheeses, fish, meat, vegetables, and pickles. The seed is also used for flavoring, and the oil is used as a scent for perfumes and soap.   J. K. K.

SEE ALSO: ANISE, CARROT, PARSLEY

Dimension
Dimension is any measurable extent, such as length, width, mass, or time. A *line* has only 1 dimension—length. A *region* has 2 dimensions—length and width. A *solid* has three dimensions—length, breadth, and thickness. Two or more dimensions are often used to calculate another measurement. *Time* and *length* are used to calculate *speed.*

Dingo
The dingo is a wild dog found in Australia. It was brought to Australia by man thousands of years ago. The dingo can be tamed as a pet.

The dingo is about 2 feet (.61 meter) high and 2½ feet (.76 meter) long. It has rough, sand-colored fur, a long bushy tail, and a head like a wolf's.

Although the tame dingo will live with other dogs and help guard sheep, the wild dingo still roves as a sheep killer. The dingo is now being hunted and destroyed as a pest.   J. M. C.

SEE ALSO: AUSTRALIA, DOG

ALLOSAURUS

TRICERATOPS

TYRANNOSAURUS

STEGOSAURUS

Dinosaur (DYE-nuh-sawr) Dinosaur is the name given to a family of large reptiles which roamed the earth millions of years before man lived. Dinosaurs were all different sizes and shapes. Some were small as rabbits; others were large as ten elephants. All dinosaurs except for one group, the *theropods,* were plant eaters. Most plant eaters walked on four legs. The large, fierce theropods walked on two. They preyed on the plant eaters. Many plant eaters were able to swim to escape; others had horns or armor to protect them. There were two main orders of dinosaurs: the *ornithischians,* with hipbones like a bird's, and the *saurischians,* with lizard-like hips.

KINDS OF DINOSAURS

Dinosaurs lived on Earth during a period of prehistoric time called the MESOZOIC ERA, which lasted about 165 million years. The earliest ancestors of the dinosaurs were the *thecodonts,* 3-foot (0.91-meter) long reptiles that ran on their hind legs. These animals were also the ancestors of the birds, crocodiles, and flying reptiles (*pterosaurs*). From the thecodonts developed the *ornithischians,* or bird-hipped dinosaurs, and the *saurischians,* or lizard-hipped dinosaurs.

Some ornithischians grew very large. They were plant eaters. The *Stegosaurs* were large dinosaurs whose back legs were much longer than their front ones. Some were about 20 feet (6.1 meters) long and 8 feet (2.44 meters) high at the hips. They had a double row of large bony plates down their back and two pairs of spikes on the end of their tail. Some people think the large bony plates helped them regulate their body temperature.

Other ornithiscians were the four-legged, armored *ankylosaurs* and the long-tailed, two-legged *ornithopods.* One ankylosaur, the *Ankylosaurus,* was a slow-moving, powerful dinosaur covered with an armor of bony plates. Its heavy, stiff tail was used for defense. The *Trachodon,* or duckbill, was an ornithopod with a mouth shaped like a duck's. *Hadrosaurs* were duck-billed ornithopods with many small teeth. Some hadrosaurs had bony crests on their head.

From the ornithopods developed the *ceratopsians,* which looked somewhat like giant rhinoceroses. They had horns and big bony fringes growing from the back of their huge heads. Some had hooked beaks for tearing the plants they ate. the *Triceratops* and the small *Protoceratops* were ceratopsians. The name *Triceratops* comes from three Greek

514

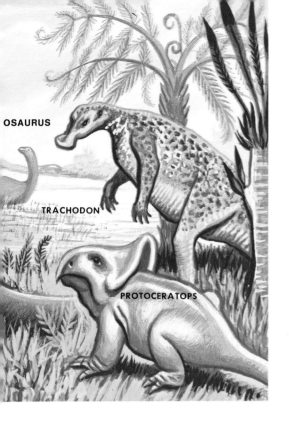

OSAURUS

TRACHODON

PROTOCERATOPS

Triceratops

Apatosaurus

Diplodocus

Stegosaurus·

words which mean "three," "horn," and "face." This strong, 25-foot (7.62-meter) animal had a short horn on its nose and a long horn over each eye.

The sauropods were huge. Apart from whales, they were the largest creatures that have ever lived. They had very long necks and tails. Some may have waded in shallow water, eating tender plants. Others may have lived on land, standing on their hind legs to eat leaves from the tops of trees. The *Apatosaurus*, the *Diplodocus*, and the *Brachiosaurus* were all sauropods.

The *Apatosaurus* was 70-80 feet (21.34-24.38 meters) long and weighed 30 tons (27.22 metric tons). It is probably the best known of the dinosaurs, with its huge body, long neck, and very small head. The *Diplodocus* was longer but weighed less. Its nostrils were on the top of its head, enabling it to breathe while almost completely submerged in water. The *Brachiosaurus*, weighing about 50 tons (45.36 metric tons) was the heaviest of all dinosaurs.

Therapods, the other group of lizard-hipped dinosaurs, were flesh eaters. They walked on two legs, the front part of their bodies inclined forward and their tails used for balance. They had fingerlike claws on their front feet with which they grasped food and long, daggerlike teeth for biting and tearing.

The largest of the flesh-eating dinosaurs

Chicago Natural History Museum

Tyrannosaurus

Allosaurus

Chicago Natural History Museum

Enmontosaurus

Chicago Natural History Museum

Protoceratops

was the *Tyrannosaurus.* Its scientific name, *Tyrannosaurus rex,* means "tyrant king of the lizards." It was 15 feet (4.57 meters) tall, had a head 4 feet (1.22 meters) long, and weighed about 10 tons (9.07 metric tons). It used its strong tail as a prop when resting and as a club when fighting. The *Tyrannosaurus* ate plant-eating dinosaurs.

THE END OF DINOSAURS

Dinosaurs roamed over most of the earth. Scientists have learned about these huge reptiles and the world in which they lived from fossils found in the earth. During the Mesozoic Era the climate of the earth was warm and mild. North America consisted of lowlands, swamps, and shallow seas. Mountains began to form toward the end of the period. Ferns, tree ferns, and conifers were the dominant plant life. The swamps were rich with vegetation. Other animals living at this time included fish, birds, snakes, crocodiles, sea reptiles, pterosaurs, and a few mammals.

The dinosaurs were among many plants and animals on land and in the oceans that had become extinct by the end of the Mesozoic, 65 million years ago.

There have been many different views as to why the dinosaurs died out. One theory stated that the dinosaurs, as *exothermic* (cold-blooded) reptiles, could not cope with the cooling of the climate. But many experts now believe that dinosaurs may have been *endothermic* (warm-blooded) like birds and mammals, and so would not have been automatically eliminated by cooler temperatures.

Other theorists speculate that mammals ate the dinosaurs' eggs or that the dinosaurs' brains were too small to insure survival. However, any theory about the disappearance of the dinosaurs must also take into account the extinction of many other animals at the same time.

Some experts think that changes in the upper atmosphere caused by the explosion of a nearby star or by a large asteroid or comet hitting the earth may have darkened the sky. The decreased sunlight would have hampered photosynthesis and greatly reduced the amount of plants at the bottom of the food chain. The animals at the top of the food chain would then be doomed.

E.R.B.

SEE ALSO: PREHISTORIC MAMMALS, REPTILIA

Dioecious (dy-EE-shuhss) Dioecious refers to types of organisms that have separate male and female individuals. In plants, this means that the female OVARY and male STAMEN are not in the same individual.

SEE: MONOECIOUS, PLANT

Diphtheria (dif-THIRR-ee-uh) Diphtheria is a sickness in which a skin or membrane grows over the inside of the throat. This grayish-green membrane may spread into the nose or extend downward to the windpipe unless prompt treatment is started. If breathing is choked off, an opening into the windpipe from the outside must be made promptly to prevent death.

The membrane usually starts to form on the tonsils one to four days after the germ which causes the disease has deposited itself.

Typical diphtheria is a sore throat accompanied by serious symptoms caused by the germs. About 10 people out of every 100 who are afflicted die, even with treatment, because of a toxin (poison) produced by the bacteria. The response to treatment with a specific antitoxin is favorable. If the type of the disease is unusually severe or is not treated promptly, malignant diphtheria develops, characterized by great swelling of the glands in the neck.

There are occasional complications from diphtheria, which, if not prevented, are very serious. One such complication is an inflammation of the heart muscle. This may cause death and is dangerous at any stage of the disease. Another complication is a PARALYSIS of the muscles because of the toxin's effect on nerves. The muscles of the soft palate are usually first affected, but such paralysis can affect the muscles of the chest or of the legs and arms.

Prevention of the disease is very important. All children should be immunized during the first nine months of life—at two, four, and six months. Then at 18 months a "booster" injection is given and is repeated before a child enters school. This program helps everybody by preventing serious outbreaks of the disease. H.K.S.

SEE ALSO: BLACK DEATH, IMMUNITY

Dippers, Big and Little see Big and Little Dippers, Ursa Major and Minor

Direct current Direct current is a stream of electrons or electric current which flows steadily, in one direction only, through a circuit. It is the opposite of *alternating current* in which the electrons move first one way, then another. Direct current cannot be changed easily from one voltage to another so it cannot be sent long distances economically.

SEE: DYNAMO, ELECTRICITY, GENERATOR

Direction finder A direction finder is a radio compass by which a ship or aircraft can find its position and direction of motion. The direction finder is equipped with a *loop antenna,* similar to one found in a portable radio. When a portable radio is turned in different directions, its volume changes. In the same way, when the loop antenna of the radio set is turned in line with a radio station, the volume is greatest. When the loop antenna is turned at right angles to the source of the radio waves, the volume is weakest.

The direction finder uses this principle of strong and weak signals. The operator rotates the loop antenna until the signal becomes strongest, and then until it becomes weakest. He reads both these bearings on an angle scale which rotates along with the antenna. The operator still does not know to which side of the station his ship or plane lies. To find the correct direction, a so-called "sense-antenna," a vertical wire antenna, is switched in. The signal picked up by this sense antenna adds to the loop signal in such a manner that the station's direction is clearly indicated. C. F. R.

SEE ALSO: BEAM, RADIO; INSTRUMENT LANDING SYSTEM; NAVIGATION

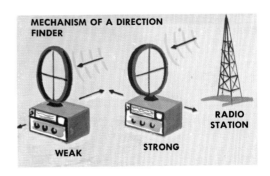

MECHANISM OF A DIRECTION FINDER

WEAK   STRONG   RADIO STATION

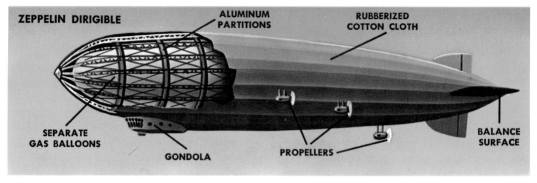

ZEPPELIN DIRIGIBLE — ALUMINUM PARTITIONS — RUBBERIZED COTTON CLOTH — SEPARATE GAS BALLOONS — GONDOLA — PROPELLERS — BALANCE SURFACE

The Zeppelin dirigibles, the most successful of the dirigibles because of their rigid frameworks, were usually filled with hydrogen gas. The use of a number of small balloons within the framework was a safety feature. If one balloon broke, the entire structure would not be affected. Large vertical and horizontal fins helped in stabilizing flight

Photo (left) courtesy Civil Air Patrol

Dirigible The term dirigible is used to describe any lighter-than-air aircraft that has an engine to propel it and which can be steered. The first dirigible flight was made in Paris, France, in 1852. Henri Giffard flew a cigar-shaped balloon propelled by a small steam engine connected to a large propeller. A crude rudder permitted limited directional control.

There are several kinds of dirigibles. The *nonrigid* dirigible, frequently called a *blimp,* uses the internal gas pressures to inflate and maintain its shape. Steel cables inside the rubberized envelope help support the control car and engines. In the semirigid modification, a structural keel is added to the bottom of the gasbag to reduce the stress and strain.

The *rigid* dirigible has a lightweight metal framework which is usually covered by a metalized fabric. Several individual gas cells or *balloonets* are located within the framework. The framework also supports the gondola, storage areas, and engine mounts. Vertical and horizontal stabilizers with movable control surfaces are located at the rear of the craft. Count Ferdinand von Zeppelin of Germany built and flew the first practical

rigid dirigible in 1900. The name Zeppelin became almost synonymous with any rigid-type airship.

All airships depend upon the buoyancy of a light gas. Hydrogen, a highly flammable gas, was used in foreign dirigibles because of its availability. Fire was a major cause of dirigible losses.

The delicate balance between the lift force of the gas and the weight of the airship is primarily maintained through the dropping of ballast and valving of gas. The power plants and horizontal control surfaces are used to aid in climbing and descending flight.

Germany used many rigid dirigibles in World War I. Zeppelins were used by the German navy to patrol water surfaces and for bombing raids.

Great interest was shown by several countries after World War I in commercial and military dirigibles. The *Graf Zeppelin* was designed to provide in-flight comfort comparable to a steamship. It was 236 meters (774.28 feet) long, 30.5 meters (100 feet) in diameter. Fully loaded it weighed 258,000 pounds (117,027 kilograms).

A series of crashes climaxed by the March 6, 1937, burning of the great *Hindenburg* during its landing at Lakehurst, New Jersey, ended the dirigible era.   R. J. J.

SEE ALSO: AVIATION, BALLOON, GAS

Disease A disease is an illness or sickness of a plant or animal. There are many kinds of diseases and many causes of them.

Communicable, or contagious, diseases are those which can be passed from sick people to well people. Chicken pox and influenza are communicable diseases. These diseases are caused by types of viruses which invade the body, usually through the nose and throat, and produce generalized infection. An EPIDEMIC occurs when many people have a contagious disease. Any epidemic was once called a "plague," but now *plague* means BUBONIC PLAGUE, a disease spread by the rat flea. In past centuries, the plague killed millions of people.

Some diseases are transmitted by CARRIERS, persons who carry the germs but do not suffer from the sickness. Mosquitoes can transmit MALARIA and encephalitis, an inflammation of the brain.

Not all diseases are caused by germs. Scurvy is caused by a VITAMIN DEFICIENCY. DIABETES is due to a malfunction of the pancreas. Mental and nervous diseases may result from hardening of the arteries of the brain or from emotional strain. Allergies are due to a sensitivity of the body to a certain substance, such as the hay fever reaction to ragweed POLLEN.

Diseases are diagnosed by the presence of symptoms, or signs of changes, in the plant or animal body. Treatment or prevention differs with the nature of the disease. Diseases can be prevented by cleanliness, STERILIZATION, disinfecting, proper food, destruction of rats and carrier insects, and quarantine of suspected CARRIERS, as well as immunization. Diseases can be treated with antitoxins, ANTIBIOTICS, HORMONES, antimetabolites (cancer-cell killing drugs), surgery, and X-irradiation.   J.M.C.

SEE ALSO: ANIMAL DISEASES, CHEMOTHERAPY, DRUGS, MEDICINE, PATHOLOGY, PLANT DISEASES

Disinfectant see Antiseptic

Dispersion Dispersion means sending things in different directions.

When applied to chemistry, dispersion can mean the uniform scattering of particles suspended in a liquid, solid, or gas. In statistics, dispersion is the scattering of various values around an average value. In optics, dispersion is the uneven bending of two or more colors that are either refracted or diffracted by a transparent, optically dense substance. One beam of a single-colored light bends to a given direction while a beam of a second color is bent to a different direction. This breaking up of light can be done with a glass PRISM. The various colors seen are called a *spectrum*. White light, because it is composed of many colors, has many dispersion angles.   M. B. C.

White light passing through a prism will be dispersed into a spectrum

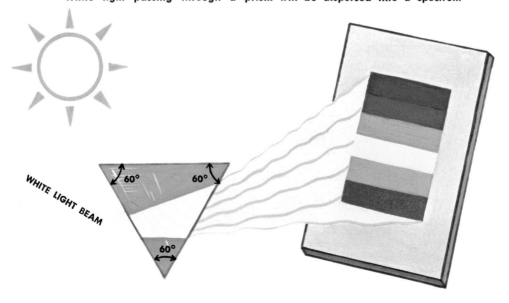

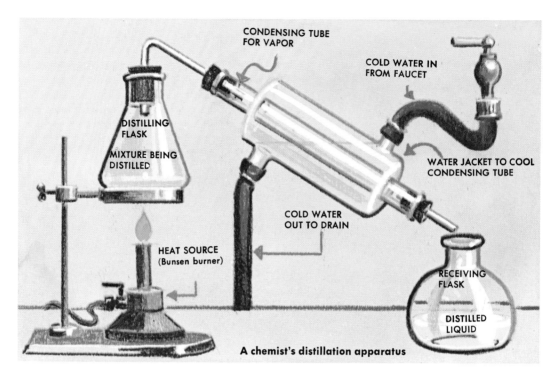

CONDENSING TUBE
FOR VAPOR

COLD WATER IN
FROM FAUCET

DISTILLING
FLASK

MIXTURE BEING
DISTILLED

WATER JACKET TO COOL
CONDENSING TUBE

COLD WATER
OUT TO DRAIN

HEAT SOURCE
(Bunsen burner)

RECEIVING
FLASK

DISTILLED
LIQUID

A chemist's distillation apparatus

Dissection (dih-SECK-shun) Dissection is the act of separating or cutting an animal body or plant into parts for the purpose of studying its structure, relation of parts or the like. In BIOLOGY, dissection means the technique of cutting through the surface of an organism and either removing or moving aside overlying parts so as to lay bare the underlying tissues or organs.

Dissociation In CHEMISTRY, dissociation is the separation of a chemical COMPOUND into simpler substances which can be recombined to form the compound again.
SEE: COMPOUNDS, STABILITY OF; ELECTROLYSIS

Distillation Distillation is a method of taking apart a mixture of different chemicals, often two different liquids. This is done by heating the mixture until one part becomes a *vapor* or *gas*. When the mixture is heated, the molecules of the liquid which has the lowest boiling temperature will be driven off most easily. The vapor formed will contain this low-boiling substance, although it may contain some of the higher-boiling substance. If this vapor is then passed through a cooled tube, it will be condensed back into a liquid. This liquid contains mostly the lower-boiling liquid of the original mixture. Most of the liquid from the original mixture that boiled at the higher temperature has remained behind.

If the liquid just distilled is put back into the distilling flask and redistilled, an even better separation can be made. In fact, if the process is repeated many times, an almost perfect separation of the two liquids can occur.

Distillation is often used to purify water. It can also be used to separate crude oil or coal tar so they can be made into useful products. The distilling process is often used in laboratory chemical RESEARCH.

Mixtures of more than two chemicals can be separated by the distillation process. When some solids or gases have been mixed together, they can sometimes be distilled. C. F. R.
SEE ALSO: CONDENSATION, EVAPORATION

Diver's palsy see Bends, Decompression

Diving see Oceanography

Diving bell see Bathysphere and bathyscaphe

Division of labor Division of labor in CELLS is the specialization of cells for different kinds of work in the body. During both individual and evolutionary development, cells change and thus bring about the efficient functioning of the body as a whole.
SEE: EVOLUTION

Dizziness This is a condition in which a person feels an unsteadiness or a whirling around. It can be a symptom of some disease. Often it is caused by disturbance in the inner ear.

DNA see Nucleic acid

Dodo The dodo was a bird that lived on the Mauritius Island in the Indian Ocean. It is extinct, which means there are no more of them. Dodoes were quite tame and could be captured.

The dodo was a large bird of the pigeon and dove family. It had no real wings and could not fly. It had short legs and could not run very fast. It probably was about the size of a turkey. It had curly, gray feathers and a long beak that was hooked at the end. Its head was partly covered with skin.

Most of what is known about dodo birds, or *drontes,* as they were sometimes called, comes from descriptions and pictures made in the 17th century. The last record of a live dodo was made in 1681. A few birds were sent to England and Holland in the 1600's. Skeletons, a head, and a foot are all that have been preserved.   C. L. K.

Dodo

ANCESTRAL DOG

JACKAL

WOLF

The ancestor of the dog probably resembled the wolf or jackal of today

Dog A dog is a domesticated mammal. For over 7,000 years, the dog has been man's close friend and servant. Dogs have been kept as pets in countries all over the world, down through civilizations from the Paleolithic period when they were first tamed by man, both for hunting and as pets.

It is almost certain that the first "dog" was a WOLF. Some scientists think that a jackal-type of animal may have been the ancestor of some of the dogs. This could be true, for the wolf and JACKAL are closely related.

The dog has a body much like that of its wild ancestor. All breeds of dogs have the same number of bones in their bodies. The skeleton is built so that the dog can move about easily on four legs. The teeth are shaped for tearing and chewing meat. Dogs have five claws on their front feet and four on their hind feet. The ears of most dogs are large and receptive to even the faintest sounds. The dog perspires through the soles of its feet and its tongue. It cannot see as well as human beings, and it does not see all colors. The dog's sense of smell is highly developed and this has made it a valuable hunter.

Mother dogs give birth to litters of puppies sixty-three days after they have been bred. They nurse their newborn for six

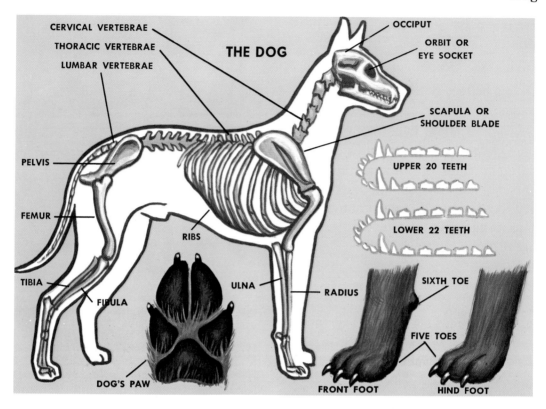

THE DOG

CERVICAL VERTEBRAE
THORACIC VERTEBRAE
LUMBAR VERTEBRAE
OCCIPUT
ORBIT OR EYE SOCKET
SCAPULA OR SHOULDER BLADE
UPPER 20 TEETH
LOWER 22 TEETH
PELVIS
FEMUR
RIBS
TIBIA
FIBULA
ULNA
RADIUS
SIXTH TOE
FIVE TOES
DOG'S PAW
FRONT FOOT
HIND FOOT

weeks. Some dogs have lived to be over twenty years old, but the average age is ten to twelve years.

Very few of the dog's wild relatives have the habit of barking, but practically all domestic dogs bark. The modern dog has many of the wild dog's instincts. It pulls its tail between its legs when it is frightened. The dog turns around in circles before lying down. This it may have inherited from the wild dog who made its beds in tall grass, which it had to trample before lying down. A dog gobbles its food and growls when someone comes near. The wild dog was always fearful of attackers when it was eating.

In the world there are several hundred breeds of dogs. They have never been so popular at any time or in any place as they are in the world today. There are over 25 million dogs in the United States today, and more than 5 million of these are pure-bred, belonging to over 100 recognized breeds. There are more breeds of dogs than of any other domesticated animals. It would take several hundred pages to describe all the breeds.

Here are the six groups of dogs with some common breeds in each group:

Collie

Courtesy Society For Visual Education, Inc.

Working dogs:
Collie
Boxer
German shepherd
Doberman pinscher
Saint Bernard

Pointer

Sporting dogs:
Springer spaniel
Cocker spaniel
English setter
Pointer
Labrador retriever

Boston terrier

Courtesy Society For Visual Education, Inc.

Fox terriers

Non-sporting dogs:	Chow Chow Bulldog Poodle Dalmatian Boston terrier

Terriers:	Airedale Kerry blue Smooth and wire-haired fox terriers Manchester Schnauzer

Dachshund

Courtesy Society For Visual Education, Inc.

Chihuahua

Hounds:	Bloodhound Beagle Dachshund Wolfhound Greyhound

Toy dogs:	Toy Poodle Pekingese Chihuahua Pomeranian Pug

By selective breeding of his stock, man has obtained just the kind of a dog he wanted for a particular purpose. The working dogs were developed to do useful outdoor work. The collie and German shepherd can work in the fields with herds of sheep and cattle. The Eskimo dogs can pull sleds, and the Saint Bernard can be trained to save the lives of travelers who might be lost in the snow.

The sporting dogs, with their keen senses, were bred to help hunters find and retrieve game. Though the non-sporting dogs are mainly pets, the dalmatian and the poodle, especially, can be trained to perform on the stage and in circuses. The hound dogs, with their highly-developed sense of smell, are useful in following the trail left by a person or an animal. Terriers were developed to pursue small animals into their burrows. The terrier is a good mouser. Toy dogs are small dogs kept as pets.

During World War II, dogs were used to carry messages to the front lines and medical supplies to the wounded, and to walk sentry duty with soldiers. The German shepherds, boxers, and Doberman pinschers are trained as "seeing-eye dogs" to guide the blind.

Man and his dog have always had deep affection for and dependence on one another. A dog will devote its life to its master. It is important for a master to give his dog proper care, training, grooming, and medical attention in order to deserve the faithfulness and love of a dog.   J. K. K.

SEE ALSO: ANIMAL DISEASES; ANIMAL INTELLIGENCE; ANIMALS, LIFE SPAN; BREEDING; WOLF

Dogbane see Wild flowers

Dogfish see Shark

Dogtooth violet see Wild flowers

Courtesy Society For Visual Education, Inc.
White flowering dogwood

Dogwood The flowering dogwood, one of the smallest but gayest trees, is decorative all year long. It is squat in shape, with a flat top. It is found all over the Northern Hemisphere.

In spring, the white or pale-pink blossoms of the dogwood appear before the leaves. Each blossom is really a cluster of yellow-green flowers, surrounded by four deeply-notched bracts which look like the petals.

In summer, the glossy, dark-green leaves add beauty to a garden. The veins are curved, running parallel to the edge of the leaf.

In fall, the leaves turn a warm crimson and bright red berries appear. The bark, which is dark reddish-brown and looks like alligator hide, and the gray flower buds make the flowering dogwood a beautiful winter tree. The wood is hard and used for shutters and door handles. J.K.K.

Doldrums (DOL-drumz) This is an area of low pressure at or near the equator. It is often called a belt of equatorial calms because winds are uncommon. In days of sailing ships, this area was avoided since ships were often becalmed for weeks.

The heated air of the equatorial region rises in great vertical currents and then descends as high-pressure air in the area of the horse latitudes. Its movement is the result of a huge convectional current caused by its steady heating at the equator. The precipitation caused by this convectional heating is both heavy and reliable. The location of the doldrums shifts as the sun's vertical rays shift during the year. H. S. G.
SEE ALSO: AIR MASSES. TRADE WINDS

Dolomite (DOLL-uh-mite) Dolomite is a mineral found in certain rocks. Some of the Alps Mountains in Europe are named the Dolomites because it was there that the French scientist, Deodat de Dolomieu, first discovered dolomite.

Dolomite deposits are found in Europe, Asia, and the United States. It is used for building and statuary. Dolomite is similar to limestone, except that it contains magnesium carbonate in addition to the CALCIUM CARBONATE in limestone [$CaMg(CO_3)_2$]. It is often found in curved crystals having a pearly-pink or white luster. Dolomite has properties similar to CALCITE, but does not react so readily when a dilute hydrochloric acid is applied. J.M.C.

SEE ALSO: MINERALS

Dolphin A dolphin is a small whale-like mammal with a long snout. Most dolphins have teeth, dorsal (back) fins and breathe through a single blow hole. These mammals belong to the same animal family as porpoises. However, porpoises are smaller and do not have long snouts or beaks. Dolphins eat mainly fish.

The playful, long-beaked common dolphins, or striped dolphins, travel in schools far out in the warm waters of the Atlantic Ocean. Their gray-striped bodies are about 8 feet (2.44 meters) long.

The gray bottle-nosed dolphin, or cowfish, which travels in schools along the Atlantic coasts, is the largest of the dolphins. It is about 12 feet (3.66 meters) long and has a short bottle-shaped snout.

The Indian river dolphin of India is blind and uses its long beak to dig in the mud for fish and prawns. D.J.A.

SEE ALSO: CETACEA, PORPOISE

Domagk, Gerhard (1895-1964) Gerhard Domagk was a German chemist and pathologist who was awarded the 1939 NOBEL PRIZE in medicine. His medical experiments with dyes began in 1930 and even-

The Doppler effect is clearly demonstrated in the way a person hears a sound nearing and passing

RAPIDLY-MOVING CAR ⟶   CAR MOVING AT SAME SPEED ⟶

tually led to his discovery of the antibacterial properties of *prontosil.*

Domagk studied thousands of azo dyes for their *chemotherapeutic* effects. In 1935 he discovered that prontosil could cure experimentally induced infections in mice. Prontosil eventually led to the development of the sulfa (infection preventive) drugs.
P.P.S.

Domestication Domestication is the process of making something accustomed to a new home. Domestication of plants and animals consists of training them to live in areas or conditions which are not native to them. A domestic animal is not wild.

Dominance Genetic dominance is physical expression of characteristics controlled by one set of GENES over those controlled by another.
SEE: HEREDITY

Donkey The donkey belongs to the same animal family as the HORSE. It is smaller and sturdier than the horse and has longer ears. There are many kinds of donkeys, found mainly in southern Asia and southern Europe. They are used as work animals.

The donkey has a short, brushlike mane and a short-haired tail with a tassel of long hair at the end. Its ears are tubular shaped, like those of the horse, but much longer. On a mountainous terrain, the sure-footed donkey is superior to the horse. It also surpasses the horse in its ability to carry heavy loads and in its life span. It has one foal at a time. Gestation takes about nine months. The donkey is in the order of odd-toed hoofed mammals.
J.C.K.
SEE ALSO: BURRO

Doppler effect (DAH-pler) Suppose a person is standing beside a road while a fast auto is passing and sounding its horn. He will notice that the pitch of the tooting horn sounds high as the car nears him. Then it will seem to grow lower after the car goes past. This is the Doppler effect as applied to moving, sound-making objects.

The pitch of a SOUND is the result of the number of air vibrations reaching a person's ear in a given time. C above Middle C is 512 waves per second, for example. But if a person is approached by such a C horn, then more than 512 vibrations per second will reach his ears—say, 540 vibrations—making the horn sound at note E above C. When the moving horn passes and moves away, fewer waves reach the ear per second—perhaps 484 waves. This gives the lower-pitch sound of B-flat.

The Doppler effect applies to changes in received waves of sound and also of LIGHT. If a fast rocket ship were aimed toward a red-colored star, it would be catching up faster with the red waves than if it were standing or moving away. Thus these waves would be shifted toward the shorter-wave range of the SPECTRUM, that is, toward the orange or yellow wave lengths. And if the space ship moved away from the star, its colors would move down to the longer wave or red spectrum area.

USES IN ASTRONOMY

Shift in position of spectrum colors is valuable to the astronomer. He uses an instrument, the SPECTROSCOPE, to detect the light wave lengths of hot objects—burning metals or hot stars. In the laboratory, any hot, light-emitting material will, when viewed through his spectroscope, give the astronomer a definite pattern of color lines—the peculiar spectrum of that material. Now in pointing his spectroscope (through a telescope) at a given star, he can recognize these same hot, light-giving elements; and will know where each spectrum line should be—if the source were standing still—relative to the earth.

However, if his observed star has all its spectrum colors shifted toward the red end of his spectroscope, for example, he figures that the star and his earth-stationed telescope are receding from each other. While if the shift is toward the blue, the star and Earth are coming toward each other. By exact measurements he can figure how fast these two celestial bodies are moving together or away.

Christian Doppler (1803-1853), an Austrian physicist, first noticed the effect in 1842. By using Doppler's principle, astronomers have discovered that some seemingly single, pinpoint stars are really double bodies. They know this because, when viewing them with their spectroscopes, the color patterns change alternately from a red shift to a blue shift in spectrum lines. By scientific deduction, this means the point of light probably is caused not by one but two stellar bodies, rotating in orbits around each other. D. A. B.

SEE ALSO: STAR, DOUBLE; STARS

Dormouse The dormouse is a small, squirrel-like rodent of the Old World. It looks like a mouse with a bushy tail. It is active at night, eating nuts and grain. It sleeps all winter.

SEE: RODENTIA

Dorsal Dorsal means "back." It usually describes a part found on or near the back of an animal, for example, a dorsal fin.

SEE: ANIMALS, CLASSIFICATION OF

Double star see Star, double

Ground doves

Mrs. Allan D. Cruickshank

Dove Doves are small, gentle pigeons. They have plump bodies and small round heads, long pointed tails, and short red or pink legs. Their feathers are soft and of delicate color. Doves live in open areas, eating berries and seeds of weeds and grasses. D.J.A.

SEE ALSO: PIGEON

Down's syndrome Down's syndrome is a disease present at the birth of about one in every one thousand babies. Victims usually have a flattened nose, upward-slanting eyes, a stocky build, and short hands. They often develop mental, visual, heart, and breathing problems. Until recently, few sufferers lived to adulthood. With improved medical care, some people with Down's syndrome now reach the age of fifty.

The English physician Langdon Down first described the disease in 1866. He called it "mongolism." In 1959, a French scientist discovered that, while healthy people have forty-six CHROMOSOMES, those suffering from Down's syndrome have forty-seven. In late 1992, trials of blood tests capable of detecting evidence of the disease in the bloodstreams of pregnant women were made by Tennessee physicians. J.H.

SEE ALSO: GENE, HEREDITY

Draco (DRAY-ko) Draco, or the Dragon, is a long line of stars that winds around the North Star and between the Big and Little Dippers.

Draco, the Dragon

At one end of the line are four stars that make the dragon's head. Because Draco is near the North Pole, this CONSTELLATION can be seen every clear night of the year.

The easiest way to find Draco is to look for the line of faint stars between the Dippers and to follow the line as it bends first toward and then away from the Little Dipper until it ends as the head of the Dragon.   C.L.K.

SEE ALSO: URSA MAJOR AND MINOR

A Chinese dragon is a symbol of goodness

Dragon Long ago people thought that huge evil monsters lived in the unknown parts of the world. These monsters were called dragons. Although they may never have existed, people believed in them and told stories about them. Dragons were usually described as huge fire-breathing lizards or snakes that could swallow men whole.

Dragons are found as symbols of evil in the ancient mythology of many countries. Dragons were slain by Sigurd, Siegfried, and Beowulf in the mythology of Norway, Germany and England. Early Christians used the dragon as a symbol of sin. However the Chinese considered the dragon as a symbol of goodness—as a god.

Fishermen, sea captains, and naval officers have reported for years having seen wild-looking monsters of the sea. Some of these descriptions can be explained away as optical illusions or mistaken identity. Other reports are from such reliable sources one may be justified in wondering if there are not some fantastic creatures as yet unclassified by man.   D. J. A.

Dragonfly   National Teaching Aids

Dragonfly A dragonfly is an INSECT of the order Odonata that lives in and close to the water. Dragonflies have long, slender, needle-like bodies with two pairs of large lacy wings that permit it to fly with great speed. The posterior pair of wings is wider at the base than the front ones. Another name for the dragonfly is "darning needle."

Dragonflies have large compound eyes that enable them to see 60 feet (18.29 meters). They eat other insects, scooping them in a "pail" made from the front of the thorax and their outstretched legs. At rest, their wings are horizontal.

The young dragonflies, called *naiads,* live underwater. They do not resemble adults. Naiads breathe through rectal gills. A long lower lip shoots out to capture prey. As the naiad grows, it sheds its skin many times.   J. C. K.

SEE ALSO: INSECTA, METAMORPHOSIS

Drainage systems see Africa, Asia, Australia, Europe, North America, South America

Dream see Sleep

Drift see Currents, ocean

Drizzle Drizzle is a fine mist-like RAIN consisting of drops of water which are smaller than 1/50th of an inch (.5 millimeter) in diameter.

Dromedary see Camel

Drone see Bees

Soil Conservation Service

In a drought, plants do not grow and animal food supplies are affected

©Parke-Davis & Company

Drug-making started with the use of herbs in ancient communities

Drought (DROWT) When there is not enough rainfall for man to grow farm crops normal to a region and to keep up the natural water supply, drought conditions exist.

The hot winds in drought regions will strip land of tons of topsoil annually, leaving them unfit for cultivation. Water holes and streams, a water source for wildlife, dry up. The leaves of trees become dry, making tracts of timber a fire hazard.

Man is constantly developing new plants which are drought resistant. He also avoids the problem by planting crops which grow fast.   H. J. C.

Drowning Death by drowning is really death by *suffocation*. This means that a person does not have enough air, or oxygen, to remain alive. The lungs have filled with water and no air can enter.

A drowning person who is still conscious may be hysterical. Since his actions are unreliable and his muscular strength is enormous (from the surplus of ADRENALIN which flows during danger), rescue is often difficult. After the victim has lost consciousness, he ceases to breathe and his limp body floats face downward.

When breathing has stopped, ARTIFICIAL RESPIRATION (mouth-to-mouth breathing) may revive the drowning victim. If the victim's heart has stopped, external cardiac massage (CPR) must also be done. These measures should continue until a victim is officially pronounced dead, because a seemingly lifeless victim could possibly be revived as long as 15 minutes after the drowning. This is because of the "drown

reflex" of some victims where the victim closes off his breathing tubes. The lungs are totally dry, and if the breathing is assisted for a while, the victim will often recover

B.M.H./E.S.S.

Drug Drugs are chemicals used in the treatment or prevention of DISEASE or defects in living things. Medicines are made from drugs. Drugs may be taken into the body by mouth; by breathing; by injections into or under the skin, into the muscles, into veins; or by insertion in the rectum. A drug may be rubbed on the surface of the skin when mixed with creams or lotions.

When a person is inoculated against TETANUS, a drug is used to *prevent* a disease; when medicine is given to a person who has pneumonia, a drug is used to *treat* a disease.

Some medicines are absorbed through the skin. Others are effective when breathed through the lungs, and are helpful in treating ASTHMA, hay fever, and some types of heart disease. Animals can be treated in much the

An ointment mill in a modern drug plant

Abbott Laboratories

A special laboratory for tablet development is used in modern pharmaceutical research

same way as humans. Plants can also be treated with drugs to prevent diseases from microorganisms and insects.

The study of the action of medicines, or drugs, is called PHARMACOLOGY. Pharmacology began to develop as a scientific study in the nineteenth century. At this time, scientists isolated substances called alkaloids from the leaves, bark, seeds, and other parts of plants. At various times in history, people have deliberately misused drugs to alter their feelings and perceptions. Starting in the late 1960s, drug abuse became a serious social problem in the U.S. and some other nations.

B.M.H.

SEE ALSO: DRUG ADDICTION, MEDICINE

Drug addiction Drug addiction is the harmful, frequent, and uncontrolled use of DRUGS. People can become addicted to dangerous but legal drugs

Antibiotic fermentation tanks

Intricate tests with bacteria in petri dishes are used to test antibacterial agents

such as alcohol, nicotine (in cigarette smoke) and many different kinds of prescription MEDICINE. Many people also become addicted to substances that are illegal under most conditions, including COCAINE, heroin, opium, and PCP, among many others.

Severe drug addiction often leads to health, behavioral, social, economic, and legal problems. As drug use increases, serious personal problems become worse, and addicts find it difficult to stop taking drugs without suffering from painful feelings of withdrawal. With medical treatment, most addicts are able to end their habit at least temporarily. Unfortunately, even after they have been hospitalized for treatment, many recovering addicts become readdicted after they are released.

In the early 1990s, U.S. law enforcement officials estimated that some seventy million Americans had taken an illegal drug at least once in their lives. Although many of these people did not develop dependencies on forbidden drugs, many Americans from all walks of life have become dependent on more socially acceptable drugs. During the late 1980s, the use of drugs such as marijuana and cocaine decreased among U.S. high school students, while the use of alcohol seemed to increase. A 1992 study indicated that, for the first time in some years, use of marijuana and LSD among high school students was increasing.

During the 1980s, physicians became increasingly aware that some prescription drugs led to legal, but nevertheless devastating, addictions. By the mid-1980s, the number of quick-acting barbiturates (a drug usually used to help people relax and sleep) prescribed by U.S. doctors was only one-fourth the number prescribed in the early 1970s.   J.H.

SEE ALSO: ADDICTION, ALCOHOLISM, CAFFEINE, MORPHINE, NARCOTICS, OPIUM, PSYCHEDELIC, TOBACCO, TRANQUILIZER

Drug habit see Addiction, Alcoholism, Drugs, Drug Addiction, Narcotics

CHERRY

PLUM

OLIVE

PEACH

ENDOCARP

MESOCARP

APRICOT

EXOCARP

A cross-section of an apricot shows clearly the parts of all drupes

Drupe (DROOP) Drupe is the name for some fleshy fruits. These fruits have one seed. This seed is closed in a very hard covering. Drupes are called *stone fruits* for this reason. Some drupes are cherries, plums, peaches, and olives.

A drupe usually consists of three parts, the *exocarp* or skin, the *mesocarp,* and the *endocarp.* The mesocarp is the pulpy part that is eaten. The endocarp is the pit or stone that contains the seed. Dates and horse chestnuts are drupes. The COCONUT is a modified drupe. The hard outer shell of the coconut is the endocarp, and the mesocarp is fibrous rather than pulpy.   M. R. L.

Dry cell see Battery

Dry ice Dry ice is the common name for carbon dioxide gas which has been changed into a solid. It is called dry ice because, at normal temperatures, the solid changes back to a gas without going through the liquid state. This process is called *sublimation.* Dry ice sublimes at a temperature of about $-79°$ C $(-110.2°$ F). Dry ice with

✳ **THINGS TO DO**

DOES DRY ICE FREEZE THINGS?

1 Never handle dry ice without wearing gloves or using a pair of tongs. The temperature of this material is —110°F. (—79°C.).
2 Place a piece of dry ice on several thicknesses of newspaper.
3 Dig out little cavities on the surface. Put mercury in one, ink in another, molasses in a third.
4 Observe what happens? Are all of the materials turned to a solid?

some liquids such as *alcohol* and *acetone* is often used to obtain temperatures as low as —110° C (—166° F).

Dry ice is manufactured from carbon dioxide gas available in the earth's atmosphere. Complicated machinery is used to compress the gas into a liquid. Then some of the confined liquid is allowed to expand and its *vaporization* freezes the remainder of the liquefied carbon dioxide.   A. E. L.
SEE ALSO: CONDENSATION, SUBLIMATION

Duckbill The duckbill (also called *platypus*) is a water-living mammal of Australia and Tasmania. It and the SPINY ANTEATER (*Echidna*) are the only mammals that both lay eggs and nurse their young. They are put in order *Monotremata*. Instead of a snout, the duckbill has skin-covered flat jaws that look like a duck's bill.

✳ **THINGS TO DO**

WILL DRY ICE SNUFF OUT A BURNING CANDLE?

1 Put several pieces of dry ice in a pitcher with a few inches of water. A cloud will form since CO_2 gas is so cold it causes the water vapor in the air to condense.
2 Now tilt the pitcher over a burning candle. The flame will go out.
3 The gas is heavier than air, tumbles over the side, and down to the blaze. As it surrounds the flame, O_2 is driven away.

Its tail is flat and its clawed feet help it in swimming and digging. Male duckbills have poison-secreting glands in their hind claws. These serve in quieting their prey and in struggles with other fighting males.

A female duckbill lays as many as three rubbery, shelled eggs, resembling those of a reptile. She deposits them in a shallow pocket dug in the stream bank. Babies, hatched in about 75 days, are soon able to care for themselves. They begin seeking food of various water insects, crayfish and worms.

An adult duckbill grows to nearly 2 feet (.61 meter) in length. The body is covered with thick, coarse fur.   I.H.S.

Duckbill (platypus)

Mrs. Allan D. Cruickshank
Mallard drake

Mrs. Allan D. Cruickshank
Mallard duck and ducklings

Courtesy Society For Visual Education, Inc.
Nest of black duck in marsh grass

Courtesy Society For Visual Education, Inc.
Ducklings of the black duck with rings around the eyes, look like the mother

Ducks A duck is a *waterfowl,* or a bird that swims. It is related to the goose and the swan but is smaller. Actually, the word *duck* means the female; *drake* is the male bird and *duckling* is the name of the young. The duck has a heavy body, short legs, webbed feet and a broad, flattened beak. Ducks are both domesticated and wild. Wild ducks are among the leading game birds and there are over forty different species found on the North American continent.

Ducks have thick plumage with an under-coat of down to protect the body from becoming wet or losing heat. Many ducks have brightly colored feathers. A duck's feathers are arranged so they are partially waterproof and oil from the gland right in front of the tail makes them even more so.

Ducks eat water plants, insects, crustaceans, shellfish and fish. All ducks which feed in the water have a sifting device in the bill which separates food from water and mud. They live in large flocks and migrate south in the fall. Some species travel from the Arctic Ocean to the tropics.

Some ducks are not built for walking. The expression, "waddle like a duck," is true. That is exactly what a duck does. Most are good swimmers and divers. Their flight can be very swift, averaging 40-50 miles (64.37-80.47 kilometers) an hour. They have great endurance for long MIGRATION flights. Their short tails prevent quick turns.

The drake is usually brighter in color while the female duck is drab for PROTECTIVE COLORATION. Many other birds lose feathers and develop bare patches on their undersides which come in contact with the

eggs and keep them at the proper temperature. A duck does the same thing by growing a special down in the spring and pulling these tiny feathers from her breast herself to insulate the nest. They also help conceal the eggs. As soon as the hatched ducklings can walk, the mother duck takes them to the water. They can swim immediately but they cannot fly for six weeks or more until their wings are strong. Many ducks are partly parasitic, caring for their own young but also laying eggs in a neighbor's nest.

Some ducks live near the sea or some large body of fresh water and dive to great depths to get their food. *River ducks,* most species of which are well-known in North America, live on the banks of rivers and

Mrs. Allan D. Cruickshank
Brightly-colored wood duck

Mrs. Allan D. Cruickshank
The scaup, a diving duck

ponds and are surface feeders. The colorful *mallard* is a river duck. *Mergansers,* or saw-bills, long-bodied ducks with rough-edged bills, feed on fish. The wild duck population is declining because their wet nesting areas are being filled in by people.

Most of the white domestic ducks prized for their meat are related to the mallard. The white *Aylesbury* and the white *Pekin* are the most popular table ducks. The *eider* duck is valuable for its down which is used in pillows and bedding. Eiderdown is harvested annually in Arctic regions.   E.R.B.

Duckweed Duckweed is a very tiny and simple plant. It grows on fresh, still water and looks like scum because it is stemless. It was named *duckweed* because ducks like to eat it.

Ductile Ductile means "able to be shaped or drawn out." When applied to METALS, ductile means "able to be hammered thin or drawn into a thin wire."

Ductless glands see Endocrine glands

Dune A dune is a small hill that is formed from windblown sand. A dune is created as the sand is blown against any obstruction, such as a rise in the ground, a boulder, or a bush.

Sand dunes are composed mainly of the mineral quartz which originates as beach sand, sandy glacial deposits, or terrace deposits from streams and rivers. Not all sand dunes contain only quartz. The White Sands area of New Mexico is composed of gypsum, and the calcite dunes of Burmuda are made from coral.

Most dunes are not stationary. They move over long periods of time. The dune migration is the result of sand being transferred from the windward side to the crest. Depending on the amount of sand available, sand dunes range in height from 1 meter (3.28 feet) to well over 100 meters (328.08 feet). Giant sand dunes can be found throughout the Sahara Desert and at the Great Sand Dunes National Monument in Colorado.

Dunes can develop into a wide range of shapes. Shape also depends on the amount of sand available, the lay of the land, restricting vegetation, and the constant direction of the winds. The principal types are *sand drifts, barchans, seifs, transverse,* and *complex* dunes. Those of the sand drift type develop in the shape of a *wind shadow* behind a rock exposure or other obstruction. The most familiar type of sand dune is the barchan. This dune forms in a crescent shape with the outer curve facing in the direction of the wind.   P.P.S.

SEE ALSO: DESERTS

Duodenum see Digestive system

Dunes in Great Sand Dunes National Monument in Colorado
Courtesy Society For Visual Education, Inc.

Dust Dust is solid matter powdered fine enough to be carried in the air. Dust is everywhere in the air in varying amounts, and consists largely of inorganic matter picked up by wind.

John R. Poss

Dust storm

Dust storm The movement of soil and other solid particles from one place to another by wind is called a dust storm. It usually happens in areas where the rainfall is light and where plant life has been removed. These regions then become *"dust bowls."*

The most significant type of soil carried by strong winds is *loess*. The plains states were stripped in the 1930's. Millions of acres of farmland were destroyed. In other sections the loss of tons of topsoil has cut the productivity of the land to less than half. Proper management is needed.   H. J. C.

SEE ALSO: DROUGHT, SOIL TYPES

Dutchman's breeches see Wild flowers

Dwarf see Cretin, Midget

Dye A substance used to stain or change the color of a material is a dye. Three thousand years ago parts of shellfish were used to color material purple. Only kings could afford clothes of such a color. Today with modern dyes, almost anyone can buy a garment of purple or red or royal blue or any color he chooses.

Color to brighten cloth, leather and

✳ **THINGS TO DO**

EXPERIMENTING WITH NATURAL DYES

1 ounce = 28.3 grams

1 pound = .5 kilogram

1 quart = .9 liter

Materials: enamel pan, rubber gloves, stirring rods (dowels or sticks), paper towels, cheesecloth, alum

1 Chop leaves, grind roots or crush berries (see suggestions below); soak overnight in enough water to cover.
2 Boil slowly for an hour.
3 Strain dye, removing plant material.
4 Add mordant (alum).
5 Dampen material, wring. Put it in dye bath to cover.
6 Simmer slowly until material is desired color. (Color will be lighter when dry.)
7 If you use one quart of berries, roots or leaves, two quarts of water and one ounce of alum, you can dye one-fourth pound of fabric.
8 Some natural dyes that can be obtained are: light brown, yellow and orange from onion skins; green from spinach; rose from beets; gold from goldenrod flowers; brown from coffee; yellow from carrots; red from red sumac berries; black from red sumac leaves.

THE ANCIENT BRITONS DYED
THEIR BODIES BLUE
WITH WOAD, A BLUE DYE

FROM A SPECIES OF SHELLFISH,
TYRIAN PURPLE WAS MANUFACTURED
IN ANCIENT PHOENICIA

AN EIGHTEENTH-CENTURY DYEHOUSE

PRESSURE KETTLES
IN A MODERN
DYE FACTORY

The dye industry has been important for hundreds of years

paper has been obtained from plants and animals since earliest time. The oldest dye known is *indigo,* a deep blue color. It came from the plant named indigo, which grew in India.

Pioneer women in colonial days used the butternut, walnut, and roots and berries of different plants to obtain dyes for their yarn and cloth.

Beginning in the mid-nineteenth century fewer simple vegetable dyes were used. The turning point came in 1856 when a young English chemist, William Henry Perkin, noted the fine dyeing properties of a chemical he had just synthesized. He had been trying to make a new chemical from the many by-products of the newly abundant COAL TAR. He called the new dye *mauve.* He and his father started a factory to produce the new synthetic.

Since then, thousands of man-made dye chemicals have been developed. By the late 1920s, even natural indigo was replaced by a better synthetic for blue-dyed textiles. Nowadays only a small percentage of commercial dyes are made from simple vegetable or mineral ones, and those few are used mainly in the dyeing of leather.

Dyeing can be as simple as a primitive housewife squeezing berries or as complex as the great factories of the modern dye industry. Whatever the case, the basic principles of dyeing are derived from definite chemical situations that can be complex.

Different dyeing methods are used for different materials. *Direct dyes* are coloring matters which dye rayon, cotton and silk from a neutral or alkaline solution without using a *mordant,* a substance that fixes color.

Dyes vary in their chemical composition and in their fastness. Vat dyes are the most lasting and produce the fastest shades. They are used for cotton, rayon, linen and wool. They are produced economically and in an infinite variety of colors. Hundreds of different types of dyes are produced.

Developed dyes are used for rayon, cotton and silk. Sulfide dyes are usually used for cottons of a solid color. Acid dyestuffs are used for silk and wool and are also used for pigment in PAINT.

Basic dyes are used for materials of animal origin—wool, silk, leather, feathers and also for viscose-process rayon. Acetate dyes are for acetate rayon and nylon. Chrome dyes are for wool, and azoic dyes are for cotton and rayon.   P. G. B.

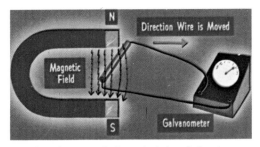

Faraday discovered the principle of the dynamo by moving a wire across a magnetic field. This is the simplest type of dynamo

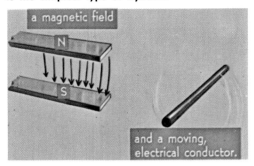

The essential parts of such a dynamo are common materials and are easily obtained

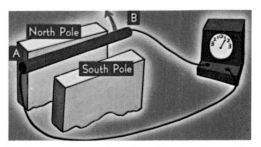

If the conductor, the wire, is moved up, the electrons flow freely through the conductor from B to A

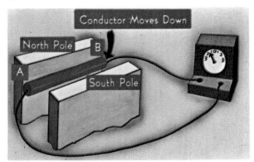

All pictures courtesy Society For Visual Education, Inc.

If the conductor is moved down, the electrons flow from A to B

Dynamics Dynamics is a branch of mechanics, the science which studies the behavior of a physical system under the influence of FORCES. This study can be divided into two parts, *statics* and *dynamics*. Statics refers to systems which are acted upon by forces but with no resulting change of motion. Pushing on a wall without having it move would be a static system. Dynamics refers to those systems which move when a force is applied to them. Pushing a chair or other object across the floor would be an example of dynamic motion.

Electricity, sound, heat and atomic physics all involve the principles of dynamics. Under the division of statics are *electrostatics,* dealing with electric charges at rest; *hydro-statics,* dealing with WATER which is not free to flow, and in MECHANICS there is a study merely called *statics,* dealing with situations such as bridge supports.

Under the division of kinetics, a more complicated study than statics, are such topics as motion, sound, and the flow of heat, electricity, and water.   A. E. L.

SEE ALSO: ELECTRICITY, HEAT, SOUND

Dynamite see Explosives

Dynamo A dynamo is a machine which makes ELECTRICITY flow through wires. Technically, a dynamo refers to a machine that produces direct electric current. Generally, however, a dynamo is an electric GENERATOR. Dynamos furnish electricity for homes, factories, street lights, trolley buses, and electric railroads. A dynamo may be as small as one's hand, or as large as a house. The size of larger dynamos is measured by the kilowatts of electricity produced. Dynamos may be run by turbines, steam engines, gasoline or even wind. A generator is used to charge an automobile battery.

Dynamos produce electricity much more economically than batteries. The dynamo does not create electrical energy, but converts mechanical energy of a turbine or a gasoline ENGINE into electrical energy.

MICHAEL FARADAY, the great English electrical physicist, discovered the principle of electrical generation. He found that if a loop of copper wire were passed between the poles of a magnet, an electrical flow having an electromotive force or voltage was created in the loop. This is the principle of *electromagnetic induction.*

To make a basic dynamo, one only needs a curved (V- or U-shaped) permanent magnet and some means of rotating a coil of copper wire between the magnetic poles. Faraday and Coulomb thought of the magnet as having *lines of force* extending between its poles, and reasoned that the work or energy of moving the coil would "cut these lines of force" and convert the mechanical energy of the moving coil into electrical energy.

The coil or wire loops make up the ARMATURE. Some current-collecting device, as a COMMUTATOR, is connected to it, and then wire brushes lead off the resulting current to do work.

Direct-current (D.C.) dynamos have now mostly been replaced by alternating-current generators. But the general principle of both types is the same. A.C. generators have the advantage that their A.C. current can be transmitted for longer distances. Also, transformers can raise and lower the voltage in A.C. systems. Direct current is still used, however, in automobiles, in electric trains and in factories that do electroplating. 　　D. A. B.
SEE ALSO: BATTERY, ELECTROMOTIVE FORCE ENERGY, INDUCTANCE COIL, MOTOR, TRANSFORMER, TURBINE

Dynamometer (dye-nuh-MAHM-uh-ter) A dynamometer is a device for measuring the TORQUE (turning force) of rotating machinery. It is often used to measure the HORSEPOWER of ENGINES or MOTORS. The rotor of the dynamometer is connected to the rotor of the machine being tested in such a way that the force causing rotation in the machinery can be measured. This force times the speed of rotation equals the POWER of the machine.

Dynamometer

Dyne A dyne (d) is a unit of force equal to the force that causes a mass of one gram to increase its velocity one centimeter per second for each second that the force is applied.
SEE ALSO: ENERGY, FORCES, MEASUREMENT

Dysentery (DISS-en-terry) Dysentery is a disease of the intestine, especially the large intestine, or *colon*. A person who has this disease loses weight rapidly and has many bloody, watery, painful bowel movements.

Amebic dysentery is caused by an AMEBA, a one-celled animal. *Bacillary dysentery* is caused by the bacillus *Shigella*. Treatment includes drugs, liquids, and careful hygiene, since germs are in the feces. 　　M.I.L./E.S.S.
SEE ALSO: DIGESTIVE SYSTEM

Dyslexia (dis-LEK-see-uh) Dyslexia is a disorder that often appears as a problem in learning to read despite sufficient intelligence and proper instruction.

Dyslexics may have difficulty understanding how words are broken down into smaller parts. The condition affects boys more often than girls. As many as twelve percent of all school-aged children may suffer from it. In 1992, Yale University Medical School researchers reported that dyslexia may come and go as students move from grade to grade. 　　J.H.

Dysprosium (dis-PRO-see-um) Dysprosium is a soft, silvery metal. It is one of the RARE EARTH ELEMENTS.

Dysprosium was discovered in 1886 by the French chemist L. de Boisbaudran. It occurs in any of several rare earth minerals such as *gadolinite* and *monazite* and was purified from these only in recent years. It has no known industrial uses but may someday prove valuable in steel ALLOYS, some of which could be used in controlling NUCLEAR ENERGY in reactors.

The pure metal rusts slowly in air to form its white oxide. Its atomic symbol is Dy; its atomic weight is 162.50; and its atomic number is 66. 　　D.A.B.
SEE ALSO: ATOM, ELEMENTS

Golden eagle

Eagle The eagle is a large, powerful bird of prey. The eagle has long stood for courage and freedom because of its size and ability to soar to great heights. The *bald eagle* is the national emblem of the United States.

The bald eagle, a native of North America, is usually found near water. Fish make up most of its diet but it also eats other small animals. Both male and female help build the tree-top nest, using large branches. The same nest is often used over and over again, with some material added each year. Nests from 12 feet (3.66 meters) to 29 feet (8.84 meters) deep have been recorded. Eagles feed by day and do not colonize. Since the eagle is so big, it needs a large hunting territory. The male measures about 32 inches (81.28 centimeters) in length; the female is slightly larger.

Young bald eagles are dark all over. It takes three or four years for them to grow their white head and tail feathers which, contrasting with the dark brownish-black body, give the adult the bald look.

The bald eagle is becoming rare. Its breeding grounds in Florida have been endangered by loss of trees due to hurricanes and real estate developments. Federal law protects it from hunters.

The *golden eagle* is found in the western United States. It is a dark brown bird with lighter markings on its tail and wingtips. It can soar higher and faster than the bald eagle, reaching speeds up to 120 miles (193.12 kilometers) an hour. It prefers ground squirrels, jack rabbits, and antelopes to fish. Some western states have laws for its protection. E.R.B.

SEE ALSO: BIRDS OF PREY

Ear The roar of an airplane, the barking of a dog, the sound of beautiful music—all cause sound waves. Ears are organs which help man and other animals to hear the sounds around them. Anything that moves back and forth makes waves. These waves hit the eardrum and start it moving (vibrating). These vibrations pass on through the other parts of the middle and inner ear until they reach the main nerve which helps animals hear. This nerve sends the message to the BRAIN. At this point the sound is "heard" by the animal.

Part of the ear tells the brain about the position of the head when it moves. Without this part, it would be difficult to keep a sense of balance.

Not all animals hear sounds with special organs. The simple animals must feel the vibrations of the water, air, or ground in which they are living. The cells on their bodies help them to know that something is moving near them. More complex animals have certain places on their bodies used only for picking up sound waves. Some insects have spots on their abdomens or legs to do this job, while most fish, amphibians, reptiles, and birds have eardrums on the surface of their heads. They have no outer ear like most mammals.

THE HUMAN EAR

The human ear is a complex organ designed to transmit SOUND waves from outside the body into the auditory nerve which leads to the auditory (hearing) centers of the brain. It is composed of an outer ear, a middle ear, and an inner ear. The outer ear, the *pinna,* is made of CARTILAGE and shaped to collect sound waves and direct them through a canal to the eardrum, or *tympanic membrane.* The canal is lined with skin possessing fine hairs, oil glands, and wax

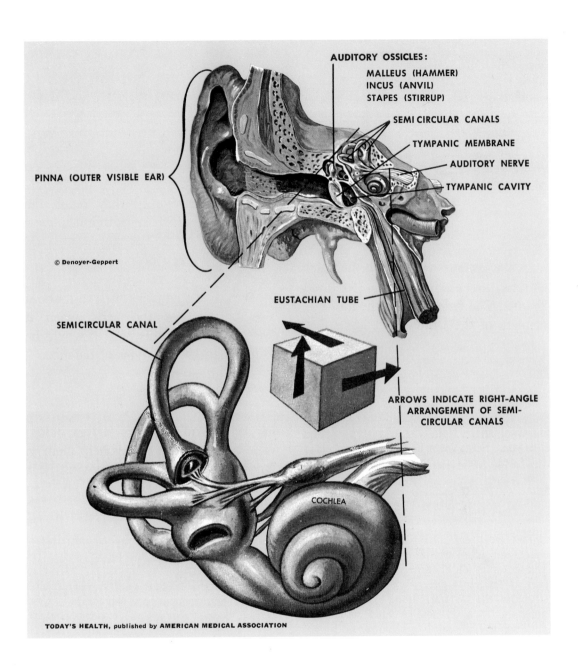

AUDITORY OSSICLES:
MALLEUS (HAMMER)
INCUS (ANVIL)
STAPES (STIRRUP)
SEMICIRCULAR CANALS
TYMPANIC MEMBRANE
AUDITORY NERVE
TYMPANIC CAVITY
PINNA (OUTER VISIBLE EAR)
© Denoyer-Geppert
SEMICIRCULAR CANAL
EUSTACHIAN TUBE
ARROWS INDICATE RIGHT-ANGLE ARRANGEMENT OF SEMI-CIRCULAR CANALS
COCHLEA

TODAY'S HEALTH, published by AMERICAN MEDICAL ASSOCIATION

glands which help to keep dirt and other materials from the eardrum.

Behind the eardrum is the *middle ear* which has two important parts, a tube leading to the back part of the mouth or pharynx, and a cavity about the size of a garden pea. The tube is called the *Eustachian tube* and is needed to equalize the air pressure on both sides of the eardrum. In the cavity portion of the middle ear are three small bones. One, called the *hammer,* or *malleus,* is attached to the eardrum. Another, called the *stirrup,* or *stapes,* fits into an oval opening in the wall between the middle and inner ears. The third bone, the *anvil,* or *incus,* lies between the other two. Vibrations striking the eardrum cause it to vibrate and set in motion first the hammer bone connected to it, then the anvil, and finally the stirrup. The movement of the stirrup stimulates the cells of the inner ear to action.

WHY ARE TWO EARS BETTER THAN ONE?

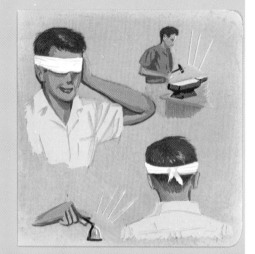

1 Find a partner to experiment with.
2 Stand in one place and close your eyes so you are unable to tell where your partner is in the room. Hold a hand tightly over one ear.
3 Have your partner make noises on different sides of you, in front, back, above, and below head level.
4 Can you tell which direction the sound is coming from?
5 Repeat again while you listen with both ears.

The outer ears of different animals

The inner ear also has two parts; one concerned with EQUILIBRIUM or balance, and the other with hearing. The hearing portion of the inner ear is a coiled, snail-like structure, the *labyrinth,* lying within a coiled bony cavity filled with a fluid called the *perilymph.* The snail-like structure, or *cochlea,* is also filled with a fluid, the *endolymph.* Sound waves are received by a group of cells (*organ of Corti*) in the cochlea. These cells are covered with fine hair-like processes called *cilia,* and make connections with nerve endings from the auditory nerve. An arm-like process (*tectorial membrane*) juts out over this group of sensory cells. The movement of the stirrup bone in the middle ear sets the perilymph in motion. This, in turn, causes movement in the fluid inside the cochlea (endolymph), which stimulates the arm-like process to move up and down upon the cilia of the sensory cells. The ciliary movement gives rise to impulses in the auditory nerve that finally reach the hearing centers of the brain.

Three looped tubes with expanded ends (ampullae) connect to a sac (utricle). The utricle connects to a smaller sac (sacculus). The tubes or semicircular canals contain endolymph which, when moving, stimulates hair cells on folds or cristae in the ampulla. Impulses sent to the brain determine the general sense of equilibrium. The saccules and utriculus contain hair cells, endolymph and calcium carbonate granules (otoliths) embedded in a gelatinous membrane. Movement of the endolymph sets the granules in motion. They strike on the hair cells to send impulses to the brain. The sacculus and utriculus determine primarily the position of the head.   J. C. K.

Eardrum see Ear, Frog

Earth Earth is the third planet nearest the sun in the SOLAR SYSTEM. It lies between VENUS and MARS. Its distance from the sun is approximately 93,000,000 miles (150,000,000 kilometers). Earth is the only planet in our solar system known to have a breatheable atmosphere, liquid water, and a temperature range capable of supporting life as we know it. The shape of this planet is not a perfect sphere, but is more nearly an *oblate spheroid*. The diameter through the poles is approximately 27 miles (43.45 kilometers) shorter than the diameter at the equator. This bulge at the equator and flattening (oblateness) at the poles is caused by the CENTRIFUGAL FORCE produced by the rotation of Earth. The distance around Earth (circumference) is approximately 25,000 miles (40,233.6 kilometers). The indirect weighing of the earth was a tremendous task but has been done with some accuracy. By scientific calculation, the weight (MASS) of Earth is approximated at 6,592,000,000,-000,000,000,000 (6 sextillion) tons ($5,980 \times 10^{18}$ metric tons).

Earth is composed of several different layers. The *core* and *mantle* make up the vast interior, and the *lithosphere* is the crust of Earth. All the water bodies (oceans, lakes, rivers, etc.) make up the *hydrosphere*. Earth is surrounded by an envelope of air that is called the *atmosphere*. The bottom of this air mass is where man lives.

The surface of the earth is composed of land and water. The land is very unequally distributed on the globe, and occupies only 30 per cent of the surface. Water covers the remaining 70 per cent of the surface. The surface of the earth is continually undergoing change. All coastlines show evidence of repeated rise and fall patterns of the land relative to the sea. Some of the change is

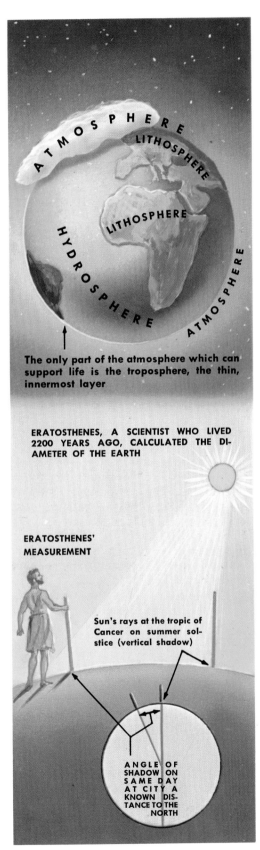

The only part of the atmosphere which can support life is the troposphere, the thin, innermost layer

ERATOSTHENES, A SCIENTIST WHO LIVED 2200 YEARS AGO, CALCULATED THE DIAMETER OF THE EARTH

ERATOSTHENES' MEASUREMENT

Sun's rays at the tropic of Cancer on summer solstice (vertical shadow)

ANGLE OF SHADOW ON SAME DAY AT CITY A KNOWN DISTANCE TO THE NORTH

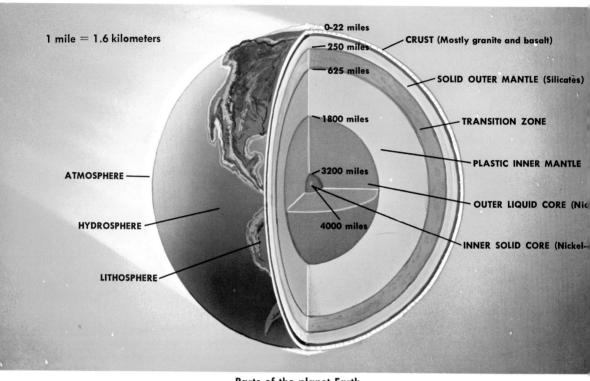

1 mile = 1.6 kilometers

0-22 miles — CRUST (Mostly granite and basalt)
250 miles
625 miles — SOLID OUTER MANTLE (Silicates)
1800 miles — TRANSITION ZONE
PLASTIC INNER MANTLE
3200 miles
OUTER LIQUID CORE (Nic
4000 miles
INNER SOLID CORE (Nickel-

ATMOSPHERE

HYDROSPHERE

LITHOSPHERE

Parts of the planet Earth

due to changes in volume of the sea. From the ocean floors, which are usually covered by sediment, rise MOUNTAINS of volcanic rocks. These may form whole mountain ranges, or just a few isolated peaks. While most of these changes occur at rates too slow to be noticed by the untrained eye, nothing is at rest, and changes are occurring constantly. Mountains are crumbling into dust, while new mountains are rising on land, due to volcanoes and sedimentation. EROSION washes land into the sea.

While the exact nature of the origin of the earth is not known, great amounts of heat must have been present. Over billions of years, some of this heat has been lost. The interior of the earth continues to give off heat, since the metallic materials that make up the core are under tremendous pressure due to gravity. Heat is also produced by radioactive materials within the crust and mantle. The most important source of heat is the sun. Without the sun, Earth would be a frozen, barren planet.

The temperatures at the surface of the earth vary greatly, depending on geographical location, season of the year, and elevation. The highest temperature (in shade) ever recorded is 136.4° F (58° C) in the Libyan Desert; the lowest is −125° F (−87.2° C)

at Vostok, Antarctica. Much of the information about Earth's interior comes from the science of *seismology*—the study of the earth's vibrations.

INTERIOR

It is known that the earth's interior contains three main divisions: the *crust*, the *mantle*, and the *core*.

Much of the crust's surface is covered by a thin layer of sedimentary rock. Beneath this are crystalline rocks, formed under conditions of high temperature and pressure. At the lower portion of the crust, a sudden change in seismic waves occurs. This may indicate a change in the composition of the rock. The rocks found in the interior have a greater DENSITY than those same rocks would have at the surface.

Based on seismic evidence and a few rare rock specimens, the mantle is believed to be made up of an iron- and magnesium-rich silicate material. This material is neither a true liquid nor a solid, but has properties similar to both. It is often called a "plastic" layer. The core consists of a liquid nickel-iron outer portion and a solid metallic interior.

The crust of the earth is operated on by thermal, gravitational, and other forces. According to the theory of PLATE TECTONICS, the crust is divided into nine major and several minor "plates" of rock. These plates move slowly over the semiliquid mantle, separating and colliding and reshaping the map of the world. New material welling up from the semiliquid interior is added to the plates at the mid-ocean ridges

ATMOSPHERE

The ATMOSPHERE, the envelope of air that surrounds the earth, is made up of several layers or divisions. The layer closest to the surface of the earth is called the *troposphere.* Its average height is about 10 kilometers (6.2 miles).

The *stratosphere* comes next, and it extends to over 50 kilometers (31.07 miles). In this layer the air is too thin to support life, and temperatures are very cold. Above the stratosphere is the *mesophere* which extends up to 80 kilometers (49.71 miles). In this layer there is very little air, and temperatures are extremely cold.

The last major layer is the *thermosphere.* Here only rocket-powered aircraft can fly, and meteor trails and AURORA displays can be seen. At the end of this layer SPACE begins. The thermosphere is often called the *ionosphere* because of the presence of highly active ions. Ions are found in high concentrations in this region.

SPATIAL RELATIONSHIPS

Earth moves around the sun in an elliptical (oval) orbit. It travels about 584,000,000 miles (939,986,890 kilometers) in circumference at an average speed of about 18.5 miles (29.77 kilometers) a second. During one revolution around the sun, Earth has rotated on its own axis 365.2422 times, causing man to experience 365.2422 days and nights. Since it is inconvenient to deal with fractional parts of the CALENDAR, a year is said to be 365 days, with one extra day added every fourth year, or leap year, making 366, to catch up with time.

Earth spins around on its own axis at a fairly constant speed. It takes 23 hours, 56 minutes, and 4.095 seconds for the Earth to make one complete rotation relative to the stars. This period is called a *sidereal day.* It takes Earth 4 minutes longer to complete a rotation relative to the sun, since it moves along its orbit at the time of rotation. This time of about 24 hours is called a *solar day.*

Earth resembles a gyroscope in its motion

The axis of the earth is tilted 23° 26′ 59″ (or about 23½°) from the perpendicular to the plane of revolution. This accounts for the changes of SEASONS and change in the length of DAY AND NIGHT. At times, the North Pole is inclined toward the sun and the South Pole is inclined away from the sun—causing summer in the Northern Hemisphere and winter in the southern. This is because the angle at which the sun's rays strike Earth—not the distance between Earth and the sun—determines the seasons. Actually, Earth is closer to the sun in winter than in summer. Midway between summer and winter, both poles are at the same distance from the sun. This occurs during spring and autumn, when every portion of Earth has 12 hours of daylight and 12 hours of night. The exact moment of equidistance is called the *vernal equinox* in the spring, and the *autumnal equinox* in the autumn.

The imaginary line drawn about 23½° south of the North Pole is called the *Arctic Circle,* and a line drawn at the same distance from the South Pole is called the *Antarctic Circle.* Similarly, the imaginary lines drawn about 23½° north and south of the equator are called the *Tropic of Cancer* and the *Tropic of Capricorn,* respectively. The zone between these two Tropics never gets cold, except on mountaintops, since the sun's rays are always overhead somewhere within this zone. Therefore, it is called the *tropical,* or *torrid zone* of the earth. The zone between each pole and its circle is called the *frigid zone,* since the sun never gets over-

As the earth spins, it moves fast in another way. It takes its moon with it and circles the sun in a solar year's time

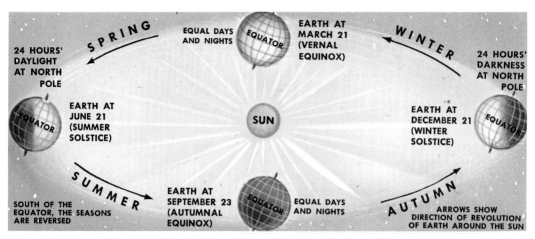

The seasons in the different hemispheres change as Earth revolves around the sun

head and there is little accompanying heat. Between the frigid and tropical zones, lie the north and south *temperate zones,* which have distinct seasonal changes.

Geographers use the equator, Tropics, and Circles to describe locations, but are able to talk about precise locations by means of additional imaginary lines called *meridians of longitude* and *parallels of latitude.*

Earth's revolution and rotation are its two main movements. However, the tilt of Earth's axis causes another strange phenomenon, *precession of the equinoxes.* This accounts for the slow change in the apparent position of the sun in the heavens at the equinoxes. Every spinning body is subject to precession or gyroscopic pull whenever any outside force tends to tip its axis out of line. Instead of tipping, the spinning body merely wobbles around its center of gravity in such a way that the ends of its axes describe circles. The gravitational pull of the sun and moon are forces that are constantly trying to straighten up the axis. Because this "righting effect" of the sun's pull is very slight in comparison with the earth's mass, the pole's motion is so slow that one circle is made in a little over 25,800 years. Thus, the North Pole now points to a different star than it did six thousand years ago.

Earth's motion is not constant. This is true with respect to both the speed of rotation and revolution. The earth's velocity in its orbit is continually changing. It has a maximum velocity at perihelion (when it is closest to the sun) and its velocity then diminishes slowly to a minimum at aphelion (when it is the farthest from the sun). The

earth has been changing its rate (speed) of rotation, sometimes speeding up, sometimes slowing down. The change is not great but it is measurable. The cause of these changes seems to be related to changes in the distribution of mass within the earth and the friction produced by ocean tides.

Earth has one natural satellite, the moon, and a variable number of man-made ones. The moon moves about Earth in an elliptical orbit. It is the gravitational attraction of the earth's mass that keeps the moon in its orbit. Earth's pulling or gravitational force also supports its atmosphere, as well as pulling objects earthward. Because of this, objects fall to the ground rather than floating off into space.

The two earliest long-lived artificial satellites are *Vanguard I,* launched March 17, 1958, and *Vanguard II,* launched February 17, 1959. The life expectancy of these artificial moons is two hundred and five hundred years, respectively.

As the moon orbits Earth, there are times when it gets in direct line between the sun and Earth. This is called a *solar eclipse* and it plunges part of the earth into darkness for about seven minutes. A much larger portion of the earth is in partial darkness where only part of the sun can be seen. A *lunar eclipse* occurs when Earth casts a shadow on the moon when Earth is between the moon and the sun.

While Earth has a gravitational attraction for the moon, the moon, too, has a gravitational pull on Earth, and is responsible for the ocean tides. The sun, also, has a gravitational pull on the earth. The tidal forces, which result from the attraction of both

The fluid core within Earth seems to flow in waves, or eddies, that create electron currents which in turn set up the magnetic fields around Earth. These magnetic fields are responsible for the working of compasses

moon and sun, have an effect on GRAVITY. Tidal motions of the earth's crust exist also, but are much smaller than the ocean tides because the earth and its interior are more rigid. The elasticity of the crust does allow tidal deformation, however.

MAGNETISM

Earth is one huge magnet, with a north magnetic pole at 70° 05′ north latitude and 93° 43′ west longitude; and a south magnetic pole about 72° 25′ south latitude and 155° 16′ east longitude. Both geographic poles are at the 90° latitudes. (Since every meridian of longitude goes through both North and South poles, the poles are at all longitudes. It is then easy to realize how far apart each magnetic pole is from its corresponding geographic pole. The magnetic poles are changing location ever so slightly. It is believed that the magnetic axis rotates about the geographic axis once in approximately every 1000 years.

Not too long ago, scientists believed that Earth's magnetism resulted from permanently magnetized iron in the deep interior. Now, with the seismic evidence of a liquid outer core, this theory has been discredited. The latest supposition is that, although Earth's magnetism does originate predominantly in the deep interior, it is due to currents flowing within the fluid outer core. These involve a conversion from mechanical energy to electromagnetic energy.   D.L.D.

SEE ALSO: ECLIPSE; EQUINOX; PLATE TECTONICS; POLES, NORTH AND SOUTH

Earth, early development of There are different theories regarding the origin of the earth. Almost all of them agree on two things—that the earth was formed by gaseous materials and cosmic dust. When these materials were brought together by gravitational attraction, great amounts of heat resulted. This took place at least five billion years ago. As the earth slowly cooled over millions of years, the heavier materials, such as iron and nickel, settled to form the core of the earth while lighter materials such as granite and basalt formed the crust. Later the continents and ocean basins formed. Gases and water vapor were given off through volcanic eruptions and eventually formed the oceans and atmosphere of today.

When the rain finally fell and retained a liquid state (rather than falling and being turned back to water vapor by the heat of the earth), the small cracks and crevices on the crust began to fill. The ocean basins originated as lower areas of the crust and are believed to have developed as a result of the buildup of the continents and continued plate tectonics. As the continents gradually eroded, thick layers of sediment accumulated at the ocean bottom, partially filling in the basins. Some scientists have suggested that the Pacific Ocean basin may represent a section of the earth's crust that was flung out into space and thus became the moon. Based on the study of rocks brought back from the moon, geologists say there is little evidence that this happened.

Water was also given off by the cooling crust and helped to form the oceans. At this time, the earth was a barren, lifeless planet. Then, millions of years ago, life first appeared in the sea. Molecules of organic material started to reproduce themselves in the form of PROTOPLASM. These first lifeforms were microscopic and very simple in nature. Millions of years passed as these simple organisms evolved into more complex structures. At the same time the nature of the seawater was slowly changing. It was becoming cooler and more saline.

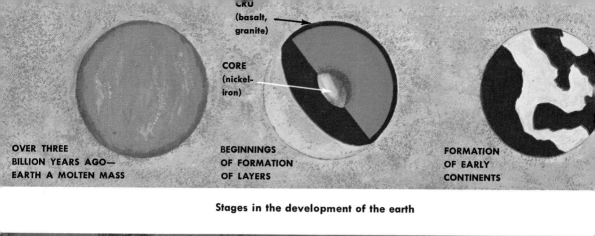

CRU
(basalt,
granite)

CORE
(nickel-
iron)

OVER THREE
BILLION YEARS AGO—
EARTH A MOLTEN MASS

BEGINNINGS
OF FORMATION
OF LAYERS

FORMATION
OF EARLY
CONTINENTS

Stages in the development of the earth

THICK ATMOSPHERE—
LITTLE SUNLIGHT

VOLCANOES

A billion years ago—warm land and sea—only microscopic life in waters

Thirty million years ago—
evolution of modern
animals

About half a billion years ago—
sunlight permits development
of green plants—early mollusks

Millions of years later, the crustal surface of the earth had grown colder. The shapes of the continents were slowly changing. In some regions crustal material was rising, creating coastlines of *emergence.* In other places the crust sank, causing the development of coastlines of *submergence.* The climates of the earth were undergoing a slow but steady change. Life in the sea continued to develop. The first green plants containing CHLOROPHYLL came into being, producing an important food source. As this development continued, both plant and animal life emerged from the sea to get a foothold on the land.

It would still be hundreds of millions of years, however, before plants would bloom and grow fruit, the club mosses develop into trees, or sea animals develop backbones and crawl upon land to live. The surface of the earth would be disrupted by earthquakes, altered by wind and water erosion and volcanic activity, and even undergo the gnawing effects of several GLACIAL AGES before it would be the surface we know today. J.H.D.

SEE ALSO: CONTINENTAL DRIFT, EARTH, GEOLOGIC TIME TABLE, GEOLOGY, PALEONTOLOGY, PLATE TECTONICS, SOLAR SYSTEM, UNIVERSE

Earthquake An earthquake is a shaking of the ground caused by sudden movement of layers of rock in the earth's crust. This movement can result from underground stresses and strains, or, indirectly, from volcanic activity. Instruments measure about six thousand earthquakes each year. Only a few are strong enough to be dangerous. The largest earthquakes can destroy whole cities.

Most earthquakes develop when cracks in the earth's crust, called *faults,* suddenly shift position. The quake is strongest at the *epicenter,* which is usually directly above the shifting fault. *Seismic shock waves,* capable of being measured with delicate instruments, may travel around the world. Seismic shocks weaken as they travel away from the quake's epicenter.

A *seismometer* detects and records earthquake shocks. It is so sensitive that it can detect vibrations that people cannot feel.

Earthquakes often occur in young mountainous areas. When they occur under the ocean floor they may cause TIDAL WAVES, such as those that struck Nicaragua and Indonesia in 1992. H.S.G./J.H.

SEE ALSO: FAULTING, GEOLOGY, MOUNTAIN, SEISMOGRAPH

Earth's crust see Earth, Geology

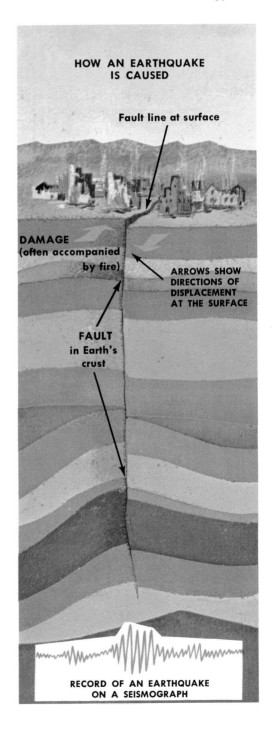

HOW AN EARTHQUAKE IS CAUSED

Fault line at surface

DAMAGE (often accompanied by fire)

ARROWS SHOW DIRECTIONS OF DISPLACEMENT AT THE SURFACE

FAULT in Earth's crust

RECORD OF AN EARTHQUAKE ON A SEISMOGRAPH

EXTERNAL VIEW

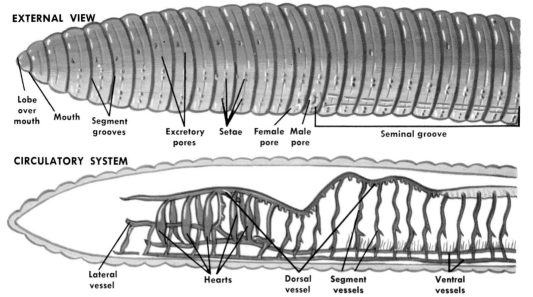

Lobe over mouth   Mouth   Segment grooves   Excretory pores   Setae   Female pore   Male pore   Seminal groove

CIRCULATORY SYSTEM

Lateral vessel   Hearts   Dorsal vessel   Segment vessels   Ventral vessels

Earthworm The earthworm helps farmers keep the soil rich and loose so plant roots can grow. Earthworms vary in size from less than 1 inch (2.54 centimeters) to 2 or 3 feet (.61 to .91 meter). As they burrow into moist soil, they swallow it, and it passes through their bodies. Later they return most of this enriched material, called *castings,* to the surface or along the channels they make.

The earthworm is the most familiar member of invertebrate phylum *Annelida.* The annelids have bodies divided into many ringlike segments called *metameres.* Most segments contain identical organs and bear external bristles, *setae,* used in locomotion. The segments are separated by thin membranes called *septa.*

The *coelom,* or body cavity, of the earthworm contains special organs for food digestion, including a crop, a gizzard and a long intestine. It has five double-tube hearts and a simple nervous system. It receives oxygen from the air through its skin. Its excretory system consists of *nephridia* in the segments.

Earthworms are *hermaphroditic,* which means that each worm has both male and female sex organs. A special gland, the *clitellum,* around the 31st to the 37th segments, receives the eggs from within the body and the sperm from another worm. The gland secretes a cocoon that holds the eggs.   J. F. B.

SEE ALSO: ANNELIDA, NEPHRIDIA, WORM

Ebony (EBB-uh-nee) Ebony is a family of trees which have a wood that is very hard and heavy. The family includes the tropical PERSIMMON tree. The best black ebony wood comes from trees in Ceylon and eastern India. The American species are lighter in color.

It is usually the *heartwood,* the firm center part of the trunk, that is used. In some trees the heartwood is streaked and in all, the wood is brittle and so is hard to work. It is used for furniture, violin finger boards, piano keys, knife handles and art objects.   D. E. Z.

Ebony tree, leaves, fruit and wood

Eccles, Sir John Carew (1903-) Sir John Carew Eccles is the Australian scientist who, with his co-workers Doctors Hodgkin and Huxley, was awarded the 1963 NOBEL PRIZE in physiology and medicine. Their research dealt with the basic transmission of nerve impulses.

Eccles first investigated the reflex properties of the spinal cord. He and his co-worker Sherrington first thought that reflex action was governed by electrical impulses, but it was shown to be a chemical transfer that brings about response in muscle fiber membrane. His later work in *neurophysiology* explained how neurons (nerve cell body) interact in integrated movements. This led to eventual understanding of the complex function of the brain.   P.P.S.

Echidna see Spiny anteater

Echinodermata (ih-kye-nuh-DER-muh-tuh) Stars belong in the sky. Dollars come from the bank. Cucumbers grow on vines and lilies bloom in fields. Stars, dollars, cucumbers and lilies are also found in the ocean. Of course, those in the ocean are different. They are all animals.

Echinoderm really means "spiny skin." It is the name of a large group of animals including starfish, brittle stars, sea urchins, sand dollars, sea cucumbers and sea lilies. A person is able to guess what these animals look like, from hearing their names.

Most echinoderms are well protected against their enemies. The body is covered with tiny calcium plates. Although the covering looks stiff, the animal is able to twist and bend. These parts are covered with two kinds of weapons—long calcium spines and tiny pincers. The spines on the sea urchin are so long that it looks like a ball of needles. Just as dust collects between the long tufts on a rug, debris could collect between these spines. When debris begins to settle on the back of an echinoderm, the pincers make it move. Only the sea cucumber has lost its calcium cover. The soft fleshy body looks

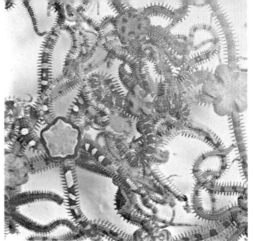

Buchsbaum

Brittle star

Buchsbaum

Sea urchin

Buchsbaum

Starfish

Buchsbaum

Sea cucumber

WATER VASCULAR SYSTEM

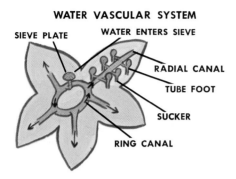

SIEVE PLATE · WATER ENTERS SIEVE · RADIAL CANAL · TUBE FOOT · SUCKER · RING CANAL

ENLARGED TUBE FOOT

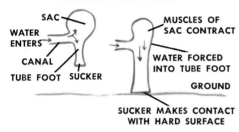

SAC · WATER ENTERS · CANAL · TUBE FOOT · SUCKER · MUSCLES OF SAC CONTRACT · WATER FORCED INTO TUBE FOOT · GROUND · SUCKER MAKES CONTACT WITH HARD SURFACE

CROSS-SECTION OF OUTER BODY WALL OF STARFISH

PINCER · COELOM · SKIN GILL · SPINE

Some important parts of a typical echinoderm

much like the skin of a cucumber. To protect themselves, some cucumbers cast out slime threads to trap the enemy.

Echinoderms have, inside their bodies, a unique system of water canals. These are useful in breathing, in catching prey and in locomotion. Water, entering a tiny pore or *sieve,* passes through an elaborate system of canals, which connect with tiny *tube feet.* Each foot has a sac at the top and a *sucker* on the bottom. As water is forced in and out, the foot alternately attaches itself to the ground as it swells and is released from the ground as it contracts. Each animal has hundreds of tube feet, which extend either through grooves or holes in the shell. When the animal is attacked, the feet may be pulled into the shell and the opening covered with spines. On sand, the feet move like legs, since the suckers are useful only on hard ground, like rock. The starfish uses these suckers in relays, to pull open the shells of clams.

Most of these animals feed on tiny organisms found on the ocean floor. The sea cucumber and sand dollar swallow great quantities of sand, from which they digest organic matter. The simple DIGESTIVE SYSTEM usually consists of a mouth on the bottom of the animal and usually an anus on the top surface. These are connected by a short, hollow digestive tube.

Echinoderms breathe through GILLS. These are often formed by finger-like or pouchlike extensions of the body wall. Sea lilies use tube feet and sea cucumbers use a cloacal tree for respiration. The thin walls of all of these provide for gaseous exchange.

The NERVOUS SYSTEM is merely a small ring of nerve tissue circling the mouth and branching into nerve cords. The circulatory system consists of a fluid which fills the body cavity and bathes the organs. Echinoderms have three distinct body layers, which form three main body areas—the digestive tube, the body cavity and the outer wall.

The sexes are separate and fertilization takes place in the water. The echinoderm larva has bilateral symmetry and a development similar to the larva of lower chordates. Scientists therefore believe that there is a close connection between echinoderms and the chordate line.   E. P. L.

SEE ALSO: ANIMALS, CLASSIFICATION OF

Echo A sound wave, traveling to a distant surface, from which it is reflected, will be heard again. This repeated sound is called an *echo.*

In order to have the reflected sound distinguishable from the original SOUND, the source of the sound must be a considerable distance from the reflecting surface. If the two are not separated by sufficient distance, the sounds will interfere with one another, resulting in a confused mixture.

Sound reflection may be both desirable and undesirable. The speed of sound is approximately 1087 feet (331.32 meters) per second at 32° F. (0° C.). This is quite slow, so it takes considerable time for sound to travel long distances. In churches and lecture halls, audiences will hear only a babble if the reflected sound of speech reaches them more than 1/20 of a second later than the original sound. This amounts to a path difference of only 50 feet (15.24 meters).

An interesting experiment is to stand at one end of an empty gymnasium and clap the hands sharply. The reflected sound of the clap can be heard quite clearly a fraction of a second later.   A. E. L.

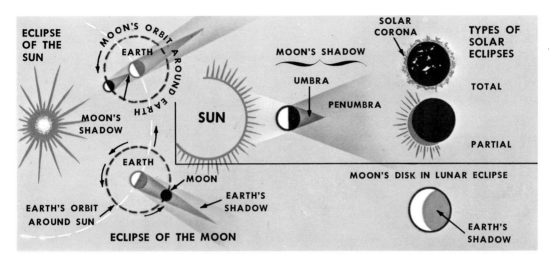

ECLIPSE OF THE SUN

MOON'S ORBIT AROUND EARTH

EARTH

MOON'S SHADOW

EARTH

MOON

EARTH'S SHADOW

EARTH'S ORBIT AROUND SUN

SUN

ECLIPSE OF THE MOON

SOLAR CORONA

MOON'S SHADOW

UMBRA

PENUMBRA

TYPES OF SOLAR ECLIPSES

TOTAL

PARTIAL

MOON'S DISK IN LUNAR ECLIPSE

EARTH'S SHADOW

Eclipse An eclipse occurs when a celestial body passes into the shadow of another celestial body. A solar eclipse occurs when the Earth moves through the shadow of the moon. An eclipse of the moon occurs when the Earth moves exactly between the moon and the sun.

In the diagram above, the line of dashes shows part of the orbit, or path, of Earth around the sun. The dotted line shows the orbit of the moon. The moon makes this trip around Earth many times a year, but Earth requires a full year to make the journey around the sun. When Earth happens to be exactly between the moon and the sun, Earth's shadow falls on the moon. This causes a *total* eclipse of the moon. The moon can still be seen as a dull red disk because of the sun's light in the earth's atmosphere.

When the moon is exactly between the sun and Earth, an eclipse of the sun takes place. Even though the moon is very small compared with the SUN, it blocks out some of the sun's rays. It can do this because the moon is much closer to Earth than the sun is. Even though it gets quite dark in a total eclipse of the sun, it is never as dark as night. Sometimes the moon is not in direct line between Earth and the sun. At such times only a part of the sun is darkened. This is called a *partial eclipse*.

People should watch only the *reflection* of the sun (as through a pinpoint hole in a box). This makes it possible to see the beautiful halo or *corona* which appears for a few seconds around the moon's disk in a total solar eclipse. Only a narrow shadow is cast by the moon on Earth, so only a few places are in the path of a total eclipse.

More common than a total eclipse of the sun is an *annular eclipse*. In an annular eclipse, the earth and the moon are in the same positions as in a total solar eclipse. However, the distance between them is greater. The moon's umbra (deep shadow) does not reach the earth. This results in a partial eclipse. When an annular eclipse is seen from some parts of the world, the moon appears to cover all but a thin outside area of the sun's *photosphere*.

As the earth and the moon revolve around the sun, shadows from both are cast into space. Since the earth is much larger than the moon, its shadow is also larger. The earth's shadow points away from the sun on the nighttime side of the earth. This shadow is made up of two parts, the total shadow, or *umbra,* and a partial shadow, or *penumbra*. The umbra is cone-shaped and extremely long. Its tip reaches into space over 800,000 miles (1,287,475 kilometers). Unlike the umbra, the penumbra widens instead of narrowing and it stretches out into space. The only phase at which the shadow of the earth can fall on the moon is at the full moon. If the earth and the moon were on exactly the same plane of orbit, one would experience a total lunar eclipse once each month. However, the moon's orbit is inclined five degrees to the earth's orbit. Therefore, a lunar eclipse occurs only if the full moon phase comes when the moon crosses the plane of the orbit of the earth, or very close to it.   O.E.Z.

SEE ALSO: ASTRONOMY

Mountain, or Alpine, environment

Barren environment

Desert environment

Courtesy Society For Visual Education, Inc.

Marsh environment

Ecology (ee-KAHL-oh-gee) Ecology is the study of how plants and animals live together and share the same ENVIRONMENT. All forms of life depend on other living and nonliving things around them. *Ecologists,* the people who study ecology, examine the relationships between living things and their surroundings. Increasingly, ecologists examine how the natural world is changed by human beings.

Ecology, a branch of BIOLOGY, is often divided into the study of three broad areas: populations, communities, and ecosystems. All the individuals of one species in a certain geographic area make up a population. Populations are often classified by their function in the environment and are referred to as producers, consumers, or decomposers. Producers are primarily green plants, which can make their own food from sunlight, air, water, and minerals. Consumers, which include animals and some plants, do not manufacture their own food. Some consumers, called HERBIVORES, eat plants. CARNIVORES eat other animals. OMNIVORES feed on both plants and animals. Decomposers, which include small organisms such as bacteria and fungi, aid in

the decay of once-living matter, which returns nutrients to the soil and water.

A group of plant and animal populations occupying the same environment is called a community. Communities can be large or small. All the plants and animals living in a tiny pond make up a community. Communities may also extend over vast areas with similar characteristics, such as forests, grasslands, or large areas of an ocean.

Ecosystems are the most complex levels of ecological systems. An ecosystem includes an entire population and all the nonliving parts of the environment that affect it, including such things as sunlight, CLIMATE, WATER, AIR, AND SOIL TYPES.

The study of ecology clearly shows how species are interdependent. The population of polar bears in the arctic region, for example, may be dependent on the number of seals found in the same community. Since seals are a primary food for polar bears, a decrease in the number of seals can lead to a smaller population of polar bears.

No species has had a greater impact on the ecosystem of earth than human beings. The growth of civilization and increasing amounts of pollution have endangered and eliminated whole populations and even ecological communities. Many governments, industries, and individuals now say they are committed to lessening ecological damage caused by people. In April 1993, U.S. President Bill Clinton and Vice President Al Gore met with representatives of the logging industry and others concerned with the vast forests of America's Pacific Northwest. The discussions were aimed at finding a way to satisfy the need for lumber for the construction industry while preserving the natural ecology of the forests.

J.H.

SEE ALSO: BALANCE OF NATURE, ECOSYSTEM, EVOLUTION, DECOMPOSER ORGANISM

Economic botany Man could not live without plant life. Food, clothing, and shelter are almost completely provided by the plant world. Economic botany is the study of all plants which help or harm other living things. Each year scientists discover new ways to use plants and their products. They also find out that more diseases and disorders are caused by them.

Green plants supply food for over a million species of animals and non-green plants. Over 90 percent of all the plant food man consumes comes from only five of the more than five hundred families of plants. Man is dependent upon plants for most of the necessities and luxuries of life. He uses them for clothing, fuel, construction,

USDA Photo

Wheat is one of the most valuable crops raised in North America.

medicine, and pleasure. Plant products have a powerful influence upon the social and economic aspects of the world.

LOWER PLANTS

Bacteria help by decomposing dead organisms, changing minerals in soil for use by green plants, retting flax, breaking down sewage, fermenting apple juice into vinegar, making vitamin B in digestive tracts of some animals, and numerous other beneficial acts. Good bacteria outnumber, by far, the bad ones. Harmful bacteria cause various diseases in animals and other plants.

Algae help by forming limestone deposits and making diatomaceous earth. It is a source of algin, used in ice cream, paint, and rubber. Some algae are used in salads, soups, or pressed into cakes. Water pollution is the greatest adverse effect caused by algae.

Fungi decompose dead things, flavor dairy products, produce alcohol, and cause bread to rise. Antibiotics, such as penicillin, aureomycin, and terramycin, are extracted from fungi. Truffles and mushrooms are examples of fungi used for food. Smut, rust, mold, and mildew are harmful plants in this group.

Economically, mosses and liverworts are of little value. They help build fertility of the soil. Sphagnum moss is used for packing. Other moss helped make peat beds now used as fuel. The greatest contribution of club moss, horsetails, and ferns is in the formation of coal deposits. A few ferns are ornamental, others are used as a vegetable in the Orient. A drug, extracted from one kind, is used to expel tapeworms.

Man has progressed in his fight against the harmful effects of lower plants. The following techniques have been proven useful: eradicating one host of fungi parasites, using antibiotics on pathogenic species, dusting infected plants with fungicides, destroying breeding places of pests, sterilizing soil and rotating crops, selecting seeds and plant

Hybrid corn is vital because of its nutritive value and the many products made from it

U.S. Department of Agriculture Photo

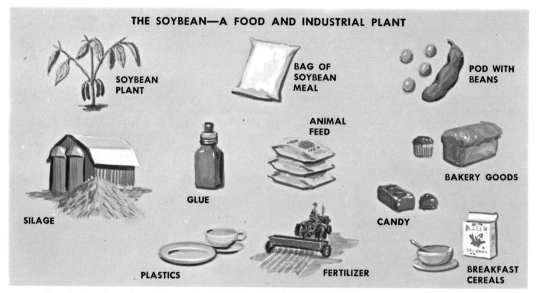

THE SOYBEAN—A FOOD AND INDUSTRIAL PLANT

SOYBEAN PLANT

BAG OF SOYBEAN MEAL

POD WITH BEANS

ANIMAL FEED

GLUE

BAKERY GOODS

SILAGE

CANDY

PLASTICS

FERTILIZER

BREAKFAST CEREALS

Hundreds of products for man's use can come from a single plant such as the soybean

stock free of disease, observing state quarantine regulations, and developing disease-resistant species.

SEED PLANTS

Some seed plants are used to make *medicine*. Belladonna is a pain-killer extracted from leaves and roots of an herb. Quinine, for treating malaria, is taken from bark of an evergreen. A local anesthetic, cocaine, is removed from coca shrub leaves. Heart disease can be treated with digitalis from foxglove leaves. Roots of monkshood yield aconite which relieves pain and fever.

Fibers, long, slender cells with a wall of cellulose and lignin, are separated from other cells, and put to many uses. Cotton comes from tiny hairs on seed coats. Rope is made from petioles of Manila hemp. Linen is woven from flax fibers. Kapok stuffing comes from tree pods, while raffia comes from the lower epidermis of palm leaves. Burlap bags and carpets are woven from jute stem fibers. Doormats and brushes are composed of coconut husks.

Seed plants are also used in *beverages*. An extract from nuts of the cola tree puts flavor in some. Coffee comes from tree beans, tea from scrub leaves, and chocolate from coca seeds. Alcohol is produced by fermenting grapes, barley, sugarcane, and other plant parts. Juice from many fruits is served as a beverage.

Seed plants are *spices*. Wintergreen, sassafras, and cinnamon are bark products. Spicy seeds include nutmeg, caraway, and mustard. Ginger, horseradish, and turmeric come from roots. Leaves furnish us with sage, parsley, and spearmint. Capers and cloves are flower buds while allspice and pepper are derived from whole fruit.

Forest products also come from seed plants. Wood is used for lumber, fuel, and paper pulp. Resin, a complex chemical secreted by trees, is used in paints, shellac, and lacquer. Rubber is latex sap taken from bark. Chicle, the basis for gum, is produced by a small evergreen. Dyes, tannins, cork waxes, sugars, and many essential oils have their origin in the forests.

Vegetables are storage areas in seed plants which are eaten. Yams and cassava are roots. White potato and asparagus are stems, while endive and lettuce are leaves. Rhubarb and celery are petioles of leaves. Flower vegetables include cauliflower and artichoke. Eggplant and tomato are "fruit" vegetables. Cereal grains, fruits, and nuts are probably the most widely used foods.

The harmful effects of higher plants center around narcotics. Morphine and codeine are drugs extracted from the opium poppy capsule. Yellow resin, taken from the dried parts of hemp plants, produces marijuana. The dangerous effects from nicotine in the dried leaves of the tobacco herb are becoming more and more apparent. These drug plants produce alkaloids which are habit forming and destructive to the physical and mental well-being of those who use them.   H. J. C.

SEE ALSO: FOREST PRODUCTS; HORTICULTURE; HYBRIDIZATION; PLANTS, MEDICINAL

Ecosystem An environment interacts with the plants and animals living in it to form an ecosystem. Everything has its own place in this system. An ecosystem may be as small as a raindrop or as large as an ocean; the organisms affect the ocean or raindrop, and in turn all the inorganic material affect the living things. Man, too, takes part in ecosystems. All of one kind of plant or animal in a given area is called a population. Many populations make up a community. A community, plus the nonliving environment surrounding it, makes up an ecosystem. Ecologists try to measure factors in the physical environment and correlate them with the number, kinds, and activities of plant and animal inhabitants present in the community.

Plants and animals make up a community within each ecosystem. The green plants convert the energy of sunlight into sugars, the source of all the energy used by themselves and other members of the community. There are animals that feed upon these plants, and other animals that prey upon the plant eaters in turn. There are thousands of these natural communities within ecosystems.

Ecosystems are not clearly defined. One runs into the next, overlapping in areas. Smaller communal systems are found within larger ones.

A tragic consequence of modern civilization is that humans have upset the natural balance of even large ecosystems. Increasing levels of pollution, growing demand for energy, and the conversion of large areas of land for nearly exclusive human use are the main factors. In the latter years of the twentieth century, limiting this damage has become a primary goal of the science of ECOLOGY.

V.V.N./J.H

SEE ALSO: BALANCE OF NATURE, PREDATOR-PREY

An example of an ocean ecosystem starts on the ocean floor where micro-organisms cause dead organisms to decay. Chemicals given off float up and supply surface organisms with raw materials for their life cycles. Phytoplankton is eaten by zooplankton which is eaten by small fish that are in turn eaten by large fish. Man then catches the large fish

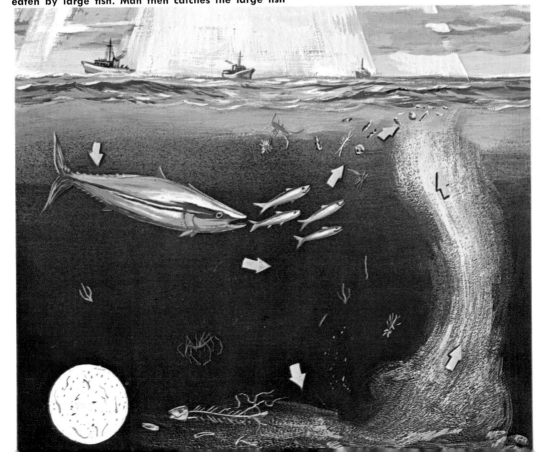

Ecotone An ecotone is the place or area where two communities meet. It may be the edge where a meadow joins a woods, the bank of a stream, or the border along a railroad track.

Plants and animals intermingle in ecotones. A wide variety of life flourishes, some from each habitat plus organisms unique to the ecotone itself. An area between a farmland and a woods may have grains growing with saplings. Shrubs that do not grow in either community appear. Poison ivy and rabbits are ecotone organisms.

In a broader sense, an ecotone is the wide belt between two BIOMES. The northern forests of conifers are separated from the tundra by an ecotone called the *tiaga* or evergreen forest. An estuary is an aquatic ecotone. H.J.C.

Ectoderm Ectoderm is the outer of the three primary germ layers formed during the early embryo development of a many-celled animal. From it come, in higher animals, the SKIN, hair, and enamel of the teeth, as well as most of the NERVOUS SYSTEM in all animals that have one. The other two layers are ENDODERM and MESODERM.

SEE. ANIMALS, CLASSIFICATION OF; CLEAVAGE; EMBRYOLOGY; EVOLUTION

Eczema (ECK-su-muh) Eczema is an inflammatory disease of the SKIN. It exists as simple, reddened spots, as groups of inflamed pimples, or elevated, moist patches. It may be progressive, beginning as a small red patch and going on to larger oozing spots that sometimes become crusted. It itches, but scratching makes it worse.

Eczema is a common skin ailment. Sometimes it starts following contact with irritating substances used in a person's work. Beauty workers, barbers, bakers, printers, and chemical workers seem to be especially affected. The irritation may come from within if a person is sensitive to certain foods. It reacts like an allergic response to something to which the body has been sensitized.

The trouble may appear anywhere on the body, but frequently on the hands, feet, legs, ears, in front of the elbows, and behind the knees. If it lasts a long time, errors in diet or repeated contacts with the same animal or vegetable substance must be investigated. An older name for eczema was "salt rheum" because it was frequently found on the hands and feet of deep-sea fishermen. Diet and exposure were probably the initial cause. H.K.S.

SEE ALSO: ALLERGY, HIVES

Edema (uh-DEAM-uh) Edema is swelling caused by an accumulation of fluid in CONNECTIVE TISSUE. It is a symptom of many diseases.

Original phonograph invented by Edison
Courtesy of The Henry Ford Museum, Dearborn, Michigan

Edison, Thomas Alva (1847-1931) Thomas Edison was an American inventor whose most important inventions were the electric light, the motion picture, the phonograph, and the stock ticker. During his career, Edison patented 1,099 separate inventions, and there were 3,000 patents bearing his name. He increased the wealth of the world perhaps more than any other man who ever lived.

Thomas Edison was born in Milan, Ohio, at a time when America was growing and developing rapidly. When he was still quite young, the Edison family moved to Port Huron, Michigan, a railroad town. It was there that young Tom began his education.

A reproduction of Edison's Menlo Park laboratory features the mercury air pump (tall apparatus in center) that was used in his incandescent electric lamp experiment

From the time he was able to talk, he asked questions of everyone he met about everything he saw.

To young Edison, his experiments were the most important part of his life. He tried to see if he could hatch goose eggs by sitting on them. He wanted to see what would happen if he set fire to his father's barn. And he experimented continuously to discover what would happen when he added one chemical to another. His consuming interests, however, gradually became electricity and COMMUNICATION.

A boy filled with initiative, Thomas Edison established business enterprises which he paid other boys to operate. He printed his own newspaper, the *Weekly Herald,* which reached a circulation of 800. As ambitious as he was, however, Edison was undependable. He would often neglect his work at hand to finish a book. During the Civil War his career as telegraph operator was made up of many positions. He was an excellent telegrapher and could always find a job, but he was unable to keep one.

At the age of twenty-one, Edison changed from an experimenter to an inventor. His first patented invention was an electric vote recorder intended to be used by legislative bodies, but it was not accepted by Congress, as it would abolish the roll call during which members could change their votes.

Although his first invention was not accepted, Edison's success was assured by his invention of the stock ticker and the sale of telegraphic devices. From that time on, he was financially independent, and could devote all of his time to his inventions. At last he began to hit his stride. He kept a cot in his laboratory at Menlo Park, New Jersey, and rested only whenever he became too tired to continue his feverish pace.

Probably the two inventions for which Edison is best known are the incandescent light (a lamp whose light is produced by incandescence of some specially prepared material such as the filament of the electric bulb) and the motion picture. Although he was ridiculed when he first spoke of these two inventions, the world has thanked "the Wizard of Menlo Park" many times over for his contributions to the world.   D. H. J.

SEE ALSO: BULB, ELECTRIC

Edison's first invention was a vote recorder

Buchsbaum

Moray eel

Eel Eels are a group of long, thin fish. Most of them live in salt water. They breathe through gills which have small openings to the outside of the body. Many kinds of eels are without the scaly covering of fish. If they do have it, the scales are very tiny. Their fins are soft.

The American eel rarely exceeds 3 feet (.91 meter) in length, though some are up to 5 feet (1.52 meters). The female eel leaves its marine habitat and swims into fresh water to mature and lay its eggs. The male eel stays behind in the salt water. Eels mature between four and ten years of age.

The *moray* is a marine eel usually living in the tropics among the coral reefs. Its leathery skin is brightly colored. The moray is a vicious savage, attacking larger animals with its sharp teeth. *Conger* eels are scaleless, marine fish that live in warm waters. The *snake* eel is the only finless fish that man has discovered at this time. The *European* eel is prized for food, although the American eel is in much less demand for human consumption.

The *electric* eel is not a true eel. It belongs in the same group as the minnows and suckers. It probably produces the strongest electric shock of any electric fish. LAMPREY EELS and vinegar eels are other species wrongly called eels.   H. J. C.

Eelworm The eelworm is a small, thread-like roundworm. Many are PARASITES of plants and other ani-

mals. They can do great damage to crops.
SEE: NEMATHELMINTHES

Efferent fibers see Nervous system

Effervescence Effervescence is the bubbling caused by the spontaneous escape of GAS from a liquid such as a carbonated drink like ginger ale.

Efflorescence (eff-loh-RESS-enns) In CHEMISTRY, the loss of water from a crystalline substance such as a SALT, is efflorescence. It results in the formation of powder on the surface of that substance. A CRYSTAL effloresces spontaneously upon exposure to the air when the water vapor pressure on its surface exceeds that of the air.

In BOTANY, efflorescence is the act of blooming or bursting into flower.

Eggplant The fleshy fruit of the eggplant is used as a vegetable. It is pear or egg-shaped. The purple *Black Beauty* variety is grown for food. Many others, with brown, green or yellow fruit, are used for decoration.

The eggplant is a tropical herb grown as an ANNUAL. It is native to India and is cultivated in the southern United States. The eggplant's stem grows slowly and cannot withstand cold. The fruit is classified as a BERRY, since the wall is fleshy and the seeds are scattered throughout. The leaves are large.   H.J.C.

Eggplant

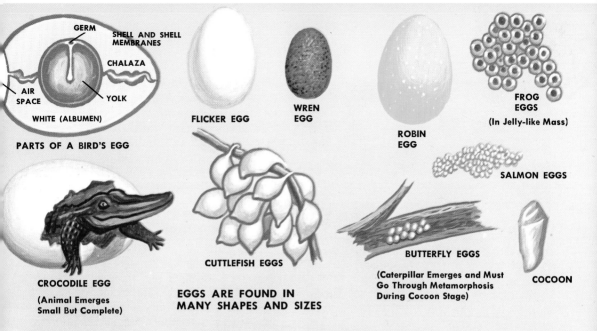

PARTS OF A BIRD'S EGG

GERM — SHELL AND SHELL MEMBRANES — CHALAZA — AIR SPACE — YOLK — WHITE (ALBUMEN)

FLICKER EGG

WREN EGG

ROBIN EGG

FROG EGGS (In Jelly-like Mass)

SALMON EGGS

CROCODILE EGG (Animal Emerges Small But Complete)

CUTTLEFISH EGGS

EGGS ARE FOUND IN MANY SHAPES AND SIZES

BUTTERFLY EGGS (Caterpillar Emerges and Must Go Through Metamorphosis During Cocoon Stage)

COCOON

Eggs There are hundreds of kinds of eggs, from robins' eggs to fish eggs to human eggs. Many living animals and plants come from eggs, or *ova,* produced in the special organs of the female. Not every egg has a shell. In some females, the egg develops in the body and the young is born alive. Mammals including humans and one family of fish are examples. In birds, worms, insects, and most fishes and reptiles, the egg or eggs are laid by the female and hatch outside the mother's body.

Eggs of all animals are similar in structure and basic elements. First, there is the germ or *nucleus* in the center which is protected in a sac of clear fluid. Around this is an outer sac of cell wall which contains a spongy network filled with a more or less transparent fluid.

The production of eggs by a female varies from one at a time, as in humans, cows, or horses, to nine million eggs laid by codfish or five hundred million produced by oysters. The only two mammals that lay eggs are the DUCKBILL and the SPINY ANTEATER.

In common usage, the egg, to most people, is a hard-shelled, oval object laid by a bird. The hen's egg is one of man's most important foods. The portion of a hen's egg commonly called the "yolk" is really the whole egg. In the surface of the yolk is the fertilized ovum. The surrounding yolk is of two kinds, white and yellow. These yolks are laid down in alternating, concentric rings around the ovum. Finally, the entire yolk mass is enclosed in a thin, elastic membrane.

As the yolky egg passes down the hen's oviduct, it revolves. As a result the heaviest or most dense portion of the white (*albumen*) is secreted around the yolky mass in spiral sheets. The ends of these sheets form short, twisted cords of white called *chalazae.*

Next, a slightly less dense layer of albumen is deposited; and finally, two thin shell membranes are laid down around the albumens. The oviduct secretes a fluid albumen which passes through the shell membranes and surrounds the denser albumens.

When an egg reaches the uterus, a shell made of calcium and magnesium phosphates and carbonates is added. At the rounded end of the egg, the two shell membranes separate to form an *air space.* The entire movement of an egg through the reproductive tract takes from 16 to 20 hours.

While bird eggshells are rarely spherical, they may be oval, cone-shaped or cylindrical. The egg shape may serve as a protective function. For instance, birds nesting upon rocky ledges or bare ground lay sharply pointed eggs that will not roll away.

Bird eggs vary widely in size and color. Eggs of a hummingbird may be less than 1 inch (2.54 centimeters) long; other birds' eggs are quite large. Eggs come in a variety of colors, with or without markings. Many eggs, when removed from the nest, appear conspicuous, but when observed in the nest, blend into the background.   J.C.K.

SEE ALSO: BIRD NESTS, EMBRYOLOGY, MAMMALIA, OVUM, REPRODUCTIVE SYSTEMS

Mrs. Allan D. Cruickshank

The snowy egret preens its feathers. The plumes on head and tail identify the bird

Egret (EE-grit) Egrets are large birds belonging to the HERON family (Ardeidae). They have long necks and legs. Their bills are long and sharply pointed. Birds in this family are wading birds and fly with their heads tucked into their shoulders.

There are two kinds of white egrets breeding in the southern United States—the American and snowy egrets. The American has black legs and feet, and a yellow bill. The snowy is a smaller bird and has black legs, but yellow feet, and a black bill. In both birds about fifty snow-white plumes grow from between the shoulders to beyond the tail. The beauty of these plumes caused the once abundant egrets to become almost extinct. Plume hunters slaughtered them.

The reddish egret occurs along the Texas Gulf. Its bill is flesh color with a black tip.

J. C. K

SEE ALSO: CRANE, HERON

Ehricke, Krafft A. (1917-1984) Krafft Ehricke was a German-American aeronautical engineer. He was one of the scientists working toward the exploration of space in manned rockets. He served as director of the program for Centaur, a high-performance, heavy-duty space vehicle, and for the Advanced Studies Department for the post-Saturn launch vehicle.

Born in Berlin, Ehricke was educated at the Technical University, Berlin, and the University of Berlin. After studying aeronautical engineering, celestial mechanics, and nuclear physics, he became a research engineer for German Army Ordnance and worked on the V-2 rocket program at Peenemunde, Germany.

Following World War II, Ehricke was one of more than one hundred specialists who came to America to work on the missile and rocket programs. In 1950, Ehricke joined the Army Ballistic Missile Agency at Redstone Arsenal, Huntsville, Alabama. In 1954 he became an American citizen, and he joined the ATLAS international ballistic missile project.

Krafft Ehricke was a member of many distinguished scientific organizations. He was a Fellow of the British Interplanetary Society, the American Institute of Astronautics, and the American Astronautical Society. He was also a member of the International Academy of Astronautics.

Ehricke was the author of many books on spaceflight. He wrote some of the entries in this encyclopedia.   M.W.C.

Ehrlich, Paul (1854-1915) A German physician and bacteriologist who founded the science of *chemotherapy,* Paul Ehrlich did early research that aided in the development of *immunology.* He shared the 1908 NOBEL PRIZE for physiology and medicine with Metchnikoff. Ehrlich's research began with the study of cell structure. He discovered that cells have an affinity for specific organic dyes. Because cells and cell granules stain differently, blood cells can be classified. Knowing this helped doctors to recognize the various types of *anemia.* This discovery marked the beginning of the science of hematology.   P.P.S.

Eider duck see Ducks

Einstein, Albert (1879-1955) Albert Einstein was a world famous physicist whose theory of relativity has completely changed man's thinking about space, time, gravitation, matter, and energy. His famous formula, $E = mc^2$ (Energy equals mass $\times$ velocity of light squared), was used to work out some of the basic problems of atomic energy. Although very few people understand it, almost everyone has heard of his theory of relativity.

Born in Ulm, Germany, on March 14, 1879, Einstein was the son of Hermann and Pauline (Koch) Einstein, Jewish merchants. They were freethinkers and Jewish traditions were not a part of Einstein's family life. Young Einstein lived a life of modest ease and luxury, but his one worry was his poor school work. As a small boy he had been unusually slow to talk, and later in school his teachers were frank in calling him "backward."

The first real spark of Einstein's genius was revealed when he was twelve years old. An older friend gave him a geometry book, which quickly became his favorite reading. He taught himself calculus and analytic geometry, and by the time he was fifteen, he knew that he would specialize in abstract studies. Unfortunately, however, his father's business failed just at that time and young Einstein was forced to train himself for a career that would enable him to become self-supporting. He decided to teach. After an unsuccessful attempt to gain admission to the Polytechnic Academy at Zurich, Switzerland, because of his poor Latin and Greek, he studied at a technical school for a year. He reapplied for admission to the Academy and was accepted. His academic record was, however, not brilliant, and he was not faithful in attending classes, a habit which later kept him from an appointment to the faculty. In 1901 Einstein married a fellow student, a Serbian girl named Mileva Marec, who was a gifted mathematician. About this same time he became a Swiss citizen. These two events were turning points in his life.

After graduation, while working as a Swiss patent officer, Albert Einstein published five important scientific papers on which he had been working in his spare time. One of these was his "Special Theory of Relativity" (1905). From this humble beginning, Einstein's reputation grew until his name became a household word. He received countless degrees, awards, and honors. Then, suddenly and terribly, he was forced to flee Berlin, Germany, where he had been teaching, because he was a Jew and

Einstein's formula, $E = mc^2$, revolutionized scientific theories about space, time, gravitation, matter, and energy.

had spoken out against Nazi torture of the Jewish people. He also was incensed because the Nazis had attacked his scientific theories on the basis of his "Jewishness." Overnight he was an exile with a price of 20,000 marks on his head. Defying the Nazis, Dr. Einstein went to France, then to Belgium, and then on to England, giving himself endlessly for the cause of the Jewish refugees. Finally he accepted an offer made him by the Institute for Advanced Studies at Princeton, New Jersey. He later became an American citizen, and until the day he died was deeply grateful to his adopted homeland.

A modest man, Einstein refused the presidency of Israel. He never owned an automobile, preferring to walk wherever he went. Money meant little to him. Next to science his great love was music, and he was a violinist of near-professional caliber. In public he was shy and retiring, but he enjoyed entertaining close friends. He was not an avid reader, preferring to think rather than read, but he greatly admired Shakespeare and Sophocles, as well as the Russian writer Dostoevsky.

Dr. Einstein was a simple man. He could not be bothered about such matters as dress and grooming. He often appeared in public without socks. His remarkable mind was so engrossed in his work that he had to simplify his rigid routine whenever possible to save every minute for thinking. No matter how busy he was, he always had time for children, and often would help them with their homework. To them his friendship was a truly cherished possession.   D. H. J.

SEE ALSO: RELATIVITY, THEORY OF

Einsteinium Einsteinium is a chemical ELEMENT. It is one of the RARE EARTH elements. Its atomic number is 99. The mass number of its most stable ISOTOPE is 254.

Einsteinium is a radioactive metal with chemical properties similar to HOLMIUM. It was discovered in 1952 after examination of material gathered by unmanned airplanes through the radioactive clouds created by the H-bomb tests at Eniwetok Island.

Einsteinium isotope 253 was recently bombarded with helium atoms in the Berkeley cyclotron to produce the element Mendelevium.

Einsteinium's symbol is Es. It is a member of the ACTINIDE SERIES. D. E. Z.

Eland see Antelope

Elasticity If a rubber band is stretched and in turn released, it returns to its original length and shape. This is an example of the physical property which certain materials exhibit called *elasticity*. Almost all materials are elastic to some extent. Steel, rubber and wood all exhibit elasticity in various degrees.

In 1676, the foundation for the theory of elasticity was laid by ROBERT HOOKE. The law, later published and named *Hooke's Law,* may be stated as: "The change in the shape of a material is proportional to the force which is creating that change."

Most materials have an elastic limit

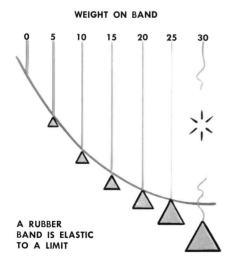

WEIGHT ON BAND

0   5   10   15   20   25   30

A RUBBER
BAND IS ELASTIC
TO A LIMIT

This law holds true only as long as a certain limit is not exceeded. This limit is called the *elastic limit* of the material. If the rubber band is deformed until it cannot recover its original shape (this usually means breaking in the case of a rubber band), it was stretched beyond its elastic limit.

When a force is applied to a piece of material, causing deformation, the internal force which tends to restore the material to its original shape is known as *stress*. The simplest forms of stress are *pressure* and *tension*. *Strain* is the change in some dimension of the body resulting from the deformation due to stress.

The ratio of stress to strain is known as the *modulus* or coefficient of elasticity. Hence, in relation to Hooke's law, it is expressed as:

$$\text{stress} = \text{modulus} \times \text{strain}$$

where the modulus here is a general term applying to any kind of elasticity.

Young's modulus, for tension; shear modulus, for shear; and bulk modulus, for volume are all examples of special formations of the above general formula expressing the modulus of materials in various shapes or for various methods of applying the stress to the material. A. E. L.

SEE ALSO: MODULUS, STRESS

Red elderberry

Elderberry Elderberry, or *elder,* is a shrub or small tree of the HONEYSUCKLE family. The common elder produces purplish-black berries used for making wines, jellies, and pies.

Electric arc welding see Arc

Electric eel see Eel

Electric eye see Electronics

Electric field see Electricity, Magnet

Electricity Electricity has become the servant and messenger of the modern world. It lights homes, runs factories and makes distant peoples neighbors. It has helped reveal the innermost secrets of the stars, the atoms, and of life itself.

Electric charge is one of those things that can be measured, thought about, and used, but cannot be defined in terms of anything simple. For, like space, time, and mass, there is nothing simpler in nature. Perhaps the best way to define it is to observe what it does. An electrically-charged object exerts a force upon another charged object at a distance. Unlike gravity, which also causes one object to attract another, charged objects may either attract *or* repel each other. Furthermore, gravity is directly connected with the mass of the objects involved, while charge and mass seem unrelated when the objects are at rest.

Experiments show that there are two different kinds of electrical charge. The first of these is called *positive* charge or "plus" charge, and is associated with the *nuclei* of the atoms of all matter. The second is *negative* or

General Electric

High-voltage power lines transmit electrical energy from power plants to cities. Such high voltage lines are necessary for use over long distances because power is lost during transmission. Cities would "stand still" if they were without electricity for a period of time

ELECTRICAL CHARGE—POSITIVE AND NEGATIVE

Two objects repel each other if both have a positive charge

Two objects attract each other if one has a positive charge and one a negative charge

Two objects repel each other if both have a negative charge

POSITIVE CHARGE	+	PLUS
NEGATIVE CHARGE	−	MINUS

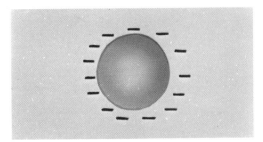

The negative charges surrounding an atom's nucleus are employed in producing electricity

"minus" charge, and is a property of all the *electrons* that surround the nucleus of the atom. In normal matter the positive charge upon the nucleus is exactly equalled by the sum of the negative electron charges that surround it.

The direction of the forces acting between charged objects depends upon the kinds of charge on those objects. For instance, if two objects have the same kind of charge, either both positive or both negative, the objects will repel each other. When each object carries a different charge, they will attract one another. This electric force of attraction, between the positive nucleus and the negative electrons, bind these to the nucleus. In a very real sense, electricity holds the world together.

The total quantity of each kind of charged particle remains practically constant in the world. Since the two kinds of charge have opposite effects, the overall normal picture is one of electrical neutrality, or apparent lack of charge. Thus, in order to observe the effects of charge in large samples of matter, it is necessary to somehow disturb the normal balance, and produce an excess of the kind of charge wanted in the object.

Many solid substances are crystalline in structure; that is, their atoms are arranged in a regular three-dimensional pattern. But in some materials, the electrons surrounding these nuclei are not tightly bound. Under certain conditions it is possible either to add or subtract a sizeable number of electrons without seriously disturbing the crystal structure. In other words, the atomic nuclei tend to remain fixed in position, but the electrons may often be moved. To give it a negative charge, one adds excess electrons.

In connection with positive and negative charge, however, one must remember that the plus and minus are signs of description, not indicators of mathematical operations, as in arithmetic or in algebra. When one sees a negative sign applying to charge, he is to remember that this merely indicates an excess number of electrons, and has nothing necessarily to do with subtraction.

CONDUCTORS AND INSULATORS

It is possible to broadly classify all matter, from an electrical standpoint, into two great groups. The kinds of matter which contain a relatively large number of free electrons which may be moved from atom to atom

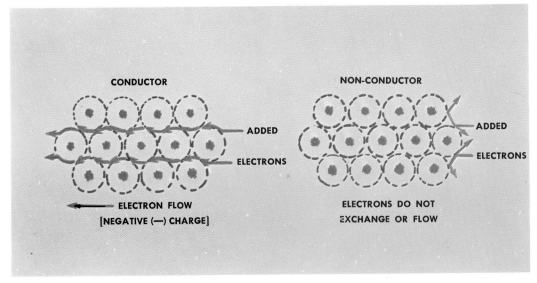

CONDUCTOR

ADDED

ELECTRONS

ELECTRON FLOW
[NEGATIVE (—) CHARGE]

NON-CONDUCTOR

ADDED

ELECTRONS

ELECTRONS DO NOT
EXCHANGE OR FLOW

※ **THINGS TO DO**

CAN ELECTRICITY BE CONDUCTED THROUGH ALL MATERIALS?

1 inch = 2.5 centimeters

1   Collect a number of items to experiment with in determining which ones will permit an electric current to flow through them.
2   Connect a light socket to a dry cell.
3   Cut a piece of wire in the middle and remove the insulation from all ends. Connect one piece to the light socket and one to the dry cell, leaving about an inch between the pieces.
4   Lay different objects across the two ends. Try cardboard, tin, a nail, coin, piece of cloth, flat stone, safety pin, etc.
5   Which ones close the circuit and permit the bulb to light up?
6   Place both ends in a glass of salt solution. What happens? Repeat in baking soda solution and in a vinegar solution.

are called *electrical conductors*. The substances within which the electrons are not free to move under moderate stress are called *electrical insulators*. Most metals are electrical conductors, as are the water solutions of the chemist's acids, bases, or salts. On the other hand, most nonmetals are electrical insulators. Of course, there is neither a perfect conductor nor a perfect insulator in existence but a number of materials serve these purposes very well in practice. For instance, silver, copper, aluminum, or even steel are often acceptable conductors, while glass, porcelain, most plastics, and dry air are good insulators.

ELECTRIC CURRENT

It is usually observed that nature acts to restore a balance of charge whenever possible. Thus, if a negatively-charged and a positively-charged object are connected together by a copper wire (conductor), the excess electrons in the negative object will tend to move through the wire toward the positive object until the charge balance in both objects is restored. This directed mass movement of electrons is called an *electric current*. The unit of current is the AMPERE. One ampere is defined as the flow of 6,250,000,-000,000,000,000 (six quintillion, two hundred-fifty quadrillion) electrons past a given

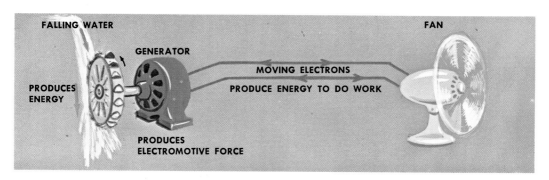

point in one second. The unit of charge, the *coulomb,* is the total charge of this number of electrons. Current strength depends upon both the number of electrons in motion and the average speed with which they move, and may be measured with an instrument called an *ammeter.*

Although the electrons in a conductor are generally free to move, they are never completely free. There is always some attraction between them and the atomic nuclei which they pass, as well as interactions between the electrons themselves. Thus, some work must be done to move electrons through any conductor. This property of interfering with the flow of electrons through it is called *resistance,* and is measured in units called *ohms.* Good conductors have little resistance, poor ones have much resistance.

If electrons are to move against this resistance, it is necessary to supply them with energy. Energy which may be converted into electron motion is called *electromotive force,* or voltage. The unit of electromotive force is the VOLT. Voltage is energy per unit of electric charge.

The three basic electrical quantities, the ampere, volt, and ohm, are related by the principle called *Ohm's Law.* This principle states that *the number of amperes which flow through any conductor is directly proportional to the number of volts applied,*

and inversely proportional to the number of ohms of resistance of the path. Thus one ampere flows through a one ohm conductor when one volt of electromotive force is applied. Electromotive force is measured with an instrument called a VOLTMETER.

Electromotive force is developed by devices called electrical generators, which act to pump the electrons through a system. A GENERATOR does not "make" electricity— electricity is already present in all matter. Rather it merely makes the electrons move. Batteries (cells) which change the energy of chemical reactions into electrical energy; and dynamos, in which an engine or turbine causes conductors to revolve rapidly in a strong magnetic field, are the most common electrical generators.

If one connects a voltmeter across any energy-consuming device, such as a light bulb, it will indicate a voltage. This voltage is equal to the electrical energy lost per coulomb of charge driven through the device by the electromotive force. This consumed energy is called the *voltage drop.* By Ohm's Law, the voltage drop is directly proportional to the resistance of the device and to the current flowing through it.

One must not think that electrons move smoothly through a wire, as water moves through a pipe. Rather, the movement is a series of impacts, in which one electron moves into a nearby atom, pushing another out. This second electron can then displace another from the next atom, and so on. Although each electron moves only a short distance, the combined movement of billions of them creates a continuous flow of charge.

Just as a moving bullet carries energy by its motion, so moving electrons carry energy with them which enables them to do useful work. In order to use and control the energy of moving electrons, an arrangement called an *electric circuit* is used.

Cells that change chemical energy into electrical energy are used in many common pieces of equipment

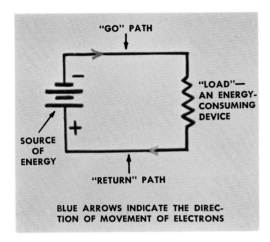

BLUE ARROWS INDICATE THE DIREC-
TION OF MOVEMENT OF ELECTRONS

The minimum essentials of an electric circuit

ELECTRIC CIRCUITS

Electric circuits take many forms, but all contain at least three basic parts: (1) a source of energy which will make the electrons move, (2) a "load" or device which will use or consume the moving electron's energy, and (3) a complete circuit, conductive "go" and "return" path for the electrons. A simple circuit containing these three parts is often called a "loop," and each of its parts, other than the conductors themselves, is called a *circuit element*. Lamps, resistors

and magnet coils are examples of circuit elements. Complex circuits, such as house-wiring systems, are made up of many such circuit elements connected in a number of simple loop circuits.

Every electric circuit has been found to follow four simple rules:

1. The number of amperes which flows is directly proportional to the voltage acting, and inversely proportional to the total resistance within the loop (Ohm's Law).

2. The number of amperes flowing in the same loop must be the same at all points of that loop.

3. The sum of the voltage drops across each part in a loop must exactly equal the voltage applied.

4. The current flowing into any point must equal that flowing out.

SERIES AND PARALLEL CIRCUITS

The various circuit elements in practical circuits may be grouped into series or parallel arrangements, or combinations of these. A *series circuit* is one in which the identical stream of current flows through each of the elements of the circuit. The applied voltage is divided among the various parts in proportion to their individual resistances. A *parallel circuit* is one in which the same voltage is applied to every circuit element.

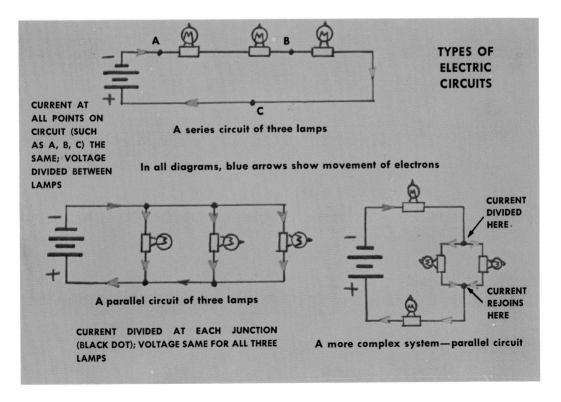

TYPES OF ELECTRIC CIRCUITS

CURRENT AT ALL POINTS ON CIRCUIT (SUCH AS A, B, C) THE SAME; VOLTAGE DIVIDED BETWEEN LAMPS

A series circuit of three lamps

In all diagrams, blue arrows show movement of electrons

CURRENT DIVIDED HERE.

CURRENT REJOINS HERE

A parallel circuit of three lamps

CURRENT DIVIDED AT EACH JUNCTION (BLACK DOT); VOLTAGE SAME FOR ALL THREE LAMPS

A more complex system—parallel circuit

A most important property of moving electrons is their ability to do useful work. And the time-rate of doing work is called POWER. The unit of electrical power is the WATT. If one multiplies the number of volts across any electrical device by the number of amperes passing through it, it is possible to calculate the number of watts of power being consumed by that device. Often the power companies will use a larger unit, called the *kilowatt*. One kilowatt is equal to one thousand watts. The electric bill which a family must pay to the power company each month is determined by the amount of electrical work which their generating plant has done in that home during the previous month. This is found by multiplying the number of kilowatts consumed by the total time that this power was used, measuring this work in energy units called KILOWATT HOURS.

Electricity and magnetism are interrelated

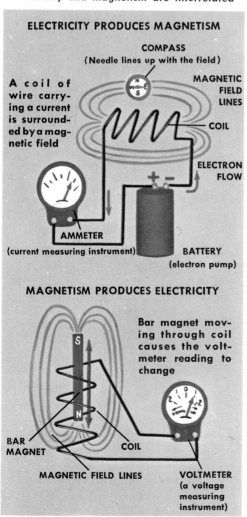

ELECTRICITY PRODUCES MAGNETISM

COMPASS
(Needle lines up with the field)

A coil of wire carrying a current is surrounded by a magnetic field

MAGNETIC FIELD LINES

COIL

ELECTRON FLOW

AMMETER
(current measuring instrument)

BATTERY
(electron pump)

MAGNETISM PRODUCES ELECTRICITY

Bar magnet moving through coil causes the voltmeter reading to change

BAR MAGNET

COIL

MAGNETIC FIELD LINES

VOLTMETER
(a voltage measuring instrument)

✳ **THINGS TO DO**

CAN ELECTRICITY SHOW A MAGNETIC EFFECT?

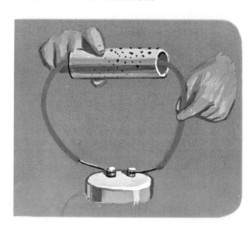

1 Insert a piece of bell wire through the center of a cardboard cylinder.
2 Connect the two ends to the terminals of a dry cell. Hold the wire up so that the circle is horizontal with the table.
3 Sprinkle iron filings on the cardboard. Notice the magnetic field formed around the wire.
4 Do not connect the wires for long, as the cell will soon be worn out.

ELECTRICITY AND MAGNETISM

The space around an electron or any other charged object seems to be in a strained condition called an *electric field*. It is this electric field which interacts with the electric fields of other charged objects and causes the mutual forces typical of such objects. But whenever electrons are set into motion, an additional new field, called a *magnetic field,* surrounds their path. The strength of this field is directly proportional to both the number of electrons moving and the velocity with which they move, or in other words, to the current. Thus if a current is passed through a suitably arranged coil of copper wire, this coil of wire will behave as a steel magnet, attracting or repelling other similar coils of wire. Winding such a coil upon an iron frame or core will strengthen the magnetic field produced. If several coils of wire are arranged upon an iron core that is free to rotate, and placed within the intense field of a set of stationary current-carrying coils, strong mechanical forces will

Whether a small electric motor (lower left) or a giant four-unit, 150,000-kilowatt generator system (above), electric power units require complex manufacturing processes, such as in making blades (upper left) and casings (below) for steam turbines

Courtesy of Allis-Chalmers Mfg. Co.

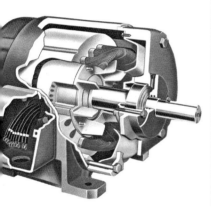

be developed. These will cause the movable coils to rotate and do mechanical work. Such a device is called an electric MOTOR. Electric motors now run all kinds of machinery, from delicate dentists' drills to the giant machines of the modern factory. There may be as many as twenty electric motors in a home—in oil burner, refrigerator, and countless other common appliances.

GENERATING ELECTRICITY FOR
HOME AND INDUSTRY

Not only does electricity produce magnetism; magnetism also produces electricity. Early in the last century it was discovered that whenever a magnetic field is changed in any way, an electric voltage is set up in the space occupied by the changing field. And if this change occurs within a coil of wire, the voltage will appear across the ends of the coil. This voltage, when active in a suitable circuit, will produce current in that circuit. This is the principle presently employed for the generation of commercial electric power in large quantities.

A set of coils are wound upon an iron core free to rotate and coupled to a powerful steam TURBINE or diesel engine. These rotating coils are placed within a framework of fixed coils, very similar to the electric motor arrangement previously described. A steady current is passed through the rotating coils to magnetize them, and the core rotated by the steam or diesel energy. As the core rotates, it causes the magnetic field within the fixed coil to change constantly, generating in it a large amount of electrical energy. This is then transmitted by a network of wiring to homes and factories.

✳ **THINGS TO DO**

CAN ELECTRICITY PRODUCE LIGHT?

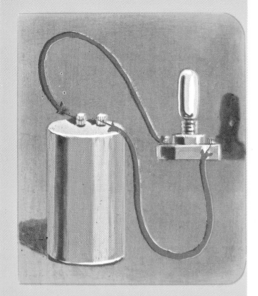

1 **Connect one end of a piece of bell wire to one terminal of a dry cell and the other end to the screw on a small light receptacle.**
2 **Repeat with a second piece of wire to the remaining posts.**
3 **The very fine filament in the bulb becomes so hot it glows and produces a light.**
4 **Would the light become brighter if a second dry cell were connected in the circuit? Try it and see.**

AC AND DC CURRENTS

In the discussion so far, it has been implied that in any given circuit, the electrons always move in the same direction around it. Sometimes the current does remain constant both in strength and direction. A system or circuit in which this occurs is called a *direct current* (abbreviated DC) system. An example of a DC system is any system powered by batteries; for instance, a flashlight, or the electrical system of the present-day automobile. However, the current need not always be in one direction. Many electrical systems are in use in which the current regularly reverses its direction of flow through the circuit. This type of system is called an *alternating current* (abbreviated AC) system. AC systems are more widely used. The most common electrical systems are AC systems

and it is upon the principles of the AC circuit that RADIO communication and modern electrical music reproduction are based.

In addition to specifying the current and voltage of the circuit, as is enough for the DC circuit, it is also necessary to specify the frequency in an AC circuit. The *frequency* measures the number of times the current changes direction in the circuit during one second. In most electrical power systems in the United States the frequency is 60 cycles per second. This means that the current flows in one direction for one one-hundred-twentieth of a second, and so on. (Of course these changes are made gradually so that the current in the circuit is constantly changing in strength as well as in direction.) Radio transmitter circuits involve frequencies in the millions of cycles, and television involves those in the hundreds of millions of cycles per second. Of course currents changing at this rate are not generated by DYNAMOS, which could never operate at the necessary speed to produce these. Instead special electronic apparatus is employed, such as the VACUUM TUBE or TRANSISTOR.

Whenever the current and voltage change, as they are continually doing in AC circuits, it is necessary to consider the effects of *reactance*. As stated, a current always surrounds itself with a magnetic field. When the current changes, so does the field. This changing field induces an opposing electromotive force back into the circuit. Thus, in an AC circuit, the driving voltage must overcome the opposition of the changing magnetic field, in addition to the ordinary circuit resistance. The opposition which the AC current experiences, due to its own changing magnetic field, is called *inductive reactance*.

Also, as seen, electrons always mutually repel each other, due to the interaction of their electric fields. Thus a moving electron in one conductor can force those in another to move, even though the two conductors are insulated from each other. And so it may sometimes appear that a changing current can flow through a perfect insulator, while a steady one cannot. (Of course no electrons actually move across the insulation, but it is their interacting electric fields that make them seem to do so.) This interesting effect is made use of in devices called *capacitors,* which are often used in AC circuitry. An AC current thus can apparently flow through

✳ **THINGS TO DO**

CAN ELECTRICITY PRODUCE HEAT?

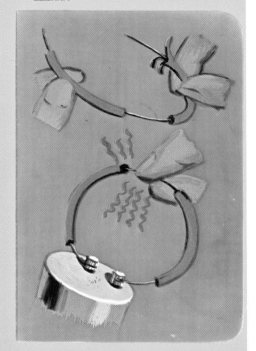

1 Remove the insulation from both ends and a section in the center of a piece of bell wire. Connect the ends to the terminals of a dry cell.
2 Place your finger on the bare wire in the center of the circle.
3 Does it feel warm?
4 Do not leave it connected too long as it wears down the dry cell.

a capacitor, but not without experiencing some opposition. The opposition to alternating current flow due to capacitor action is called *capacitative reactance*. The total inductive reactance, capacitative reactance, and resistance of a circuit is called its *impedance*.

By controlling the amount of inductive and capacitative reactance in a circuit, one may observe some interesting effects. One of the most important of these is called *resonance*. Here the circuit may be made to respond strongly to an AC current of one particular frequency, while largely ignoring those of other frequencies which may also be present. It is by the use of resonance that people are able to tune radio or television receivers to one particular broadcasting station, and exclude others.

TRANSFORMERS

The practical advantage of AC systems is primarily that changing voltages may readily be stepped either up or down by use of a device called a *transformer*. A TRANSFORMER is simply two separate, isolated coils of wire wound on the same magnetic iron core. An AC current flowing in the first coil produces a changing magnetic field in the core and induces an AC voltage into the second coil. By suitably arranging the size of the core and the number of turns on the coils, it is possible to step up or step down voltages at will. Thus the transformer permits the use of a relatively low voltage, for safety's sake, within the home, yet allowing it to be transmitted from a distant power plant at a much higher voltage. One may use a transformer to step-down the voltage for operating doorbells, electric toys, and other small appliances. A transformer cannot be used on a direct-current circuit, since the current, and thus the magnetic field involved, does not change.

ELECTRICITY AS RADIO WAVES

When the frequency is high enough an alternating current may be supplied to a suitable ANTENNA, which will then radiate electromagnetic waves in space. These waves are interlocking magnetic and electric fields which spread out from the antenna and can carry telegraph, voice, or picture signals to great distances. This is the basis of modern RADIO and TELEVISION.

When necessary, AC voltages may be easily converted to steady DC by the use of a *rectifier*. It is more difficult and expensive to transform DC into AC when desired, particularly for high-power applications.

In the electrochemical industries, for instance in the manufacture of aluminum, magnesium, or copper, direct current is essential. The basic current supply for most radio, television, or other electronic equipment must also be DC at the present time. So DC circuits will have their uses.

OTHER SOURCES OF ELECTRICITY

A *fuel cell* is a device used to produce electricity from a chemical reaction, usually the combination of hydrogen and oxygen. Fuel cells have been used in space exploration vehicles.

Some devices are used to generate very small amounts of electricity. A *thermocouple* is two different metals in contact with each

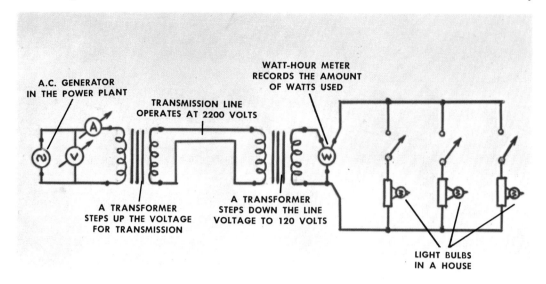

A simplified power system wiring diagram showing use of the schematic symbols

other. When the junction is heated, a current flows out of it. Thermocouples are usually used to measure temperature. *Photosensitive* materials emit electrons when struck by light. These materials are used to make solar cells that switch streetlights on when sunlight disappears, and to make cameras that automatically adjust exposures to differing amounts of light. *Piezoelectric crystals,* such as quartz and Rochelle salt, produce a small current when compressed. They are used in hearing aids, telephones, and microphones.

Throughout the late twentieth century, new methods of generating large amounts of electricity suitable for industrial, commercial, and home use have been explored. By the mid-1990s, however, nearly all of the world's high-amperage electricity was still being generated from FOSSIL FUELS, HYDRO-ELECTRIC POWER, and NUCLEAR ENERGY. Alternative sources of energy that can be converted to electricity include solar power, wind power, geothermal power, and synthetic fuels. Despite large-scale experiments, all of these alternatives still face economic and psychological obstacles. Concerns over fossil fuel shortages and pollution caused by fossil fuel burning and nuclear waste will probably result in a gradual growth of experimental and practical alternative sources of electricity.   C.F.R./J.H.

SEE ALSO: ATOM, BATTERY, ELECTROCHEMIS-TRY, ELECTRON, ELECTRON BORROWING, ELECTRONICS, ENERGY, MAGNET, OHM, PHOTO-ELECTRICITY, PIEZOELECTRIC EFFECT, STATIC ELECTRICITY, THERMOELECTRICITY

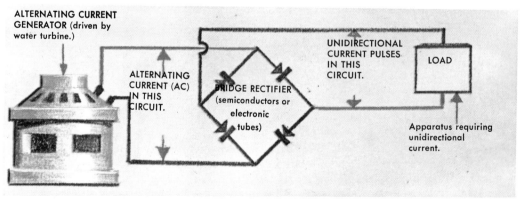

Alternating current is changed into series of unidirectional current pulses by means of a rectifier.

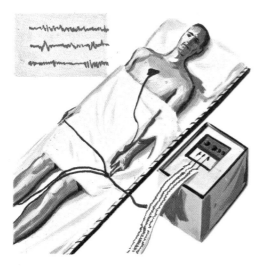

Electrodes of an EKG are placed at various points to record differences in circulation

Electrocardiograph The electrocardiograph is an electrical instrument which records the activity of the heart muscle. As the HEART beats, several activities take place in a regular order. The electrocardiograph records changes that occur in a complete heart beat. This record of varying electrical action is called an *electrocardiogram.*

Doctors who are heart specialists use these records, known as ECG or EKG. They are a great help in studying the irregular heart. The EKG looks like a line graph with high and low points occurring at regular intervals along a wavy line. There is a pattern of these lines which is repeated many times. If the pattern shows great differences from the pattern of the normal heart, doctors make a scientific analysis of the electrocardiogram. They can discover which part of the heart is not working properly, and this knowledge may lead them to a solution of the heart patient's problem.

The electrocardiograph machine records deflection time and sustained response to direct current voltage. The ELECTRODES are attached to various parts of the body. There is no pain or shock to the patient at any time. Some electrodes are placed near the heart, while others are fastened to the arm, leg and the neck. This is done to register differences in heart action and the circulation of the blood. These data become the basis of medical interpretation.

In a normal electrocardiogram, a small low-voltage change is caused by the contraction of the auricles of the heart. This is called the *P* wave. A resting space is indicated when the blood moves from the auricles to the ventricles of the heart. This segment on the graph is known as the *PR*. Then rapid, tall signals, known as the *QRS* group, follow immediately. They show excitement of the ventricles. As the ventricles return to a relaxed state, a *T* wave is visible in the slow, smoother line. This cycle of waves is repeated and the variations noted.   D. E. Z.
SEE ALSO: CIRCULATORY SYSTEM

Electrochemistry Many chemical reactions can be caused by passing an electric current through a substance. Some chemical reactions will produce electrical energy. These are *electrochemical reactions.*

ALESSANDRO VOLTA, an Italian physics professor, discovered that when two different METALS were put in a water solution which contained a SALT of these metals (or any other salt, acid or alkali), an electric current could occur. A direct result of this discovery was the invention of the familiar BATTERY.

If a battery is constructed by placing a strip of zinc metal and one of copper in a dilute solution of sulfuric acid, an electric current will flow if the strips, called plates, are connected by a wire. The zinc is eaten away. Both changes are evidence of the conversion of chemical energy into electrical energy. In obtaining this electrical energy the zinc plate is dissolved and gases are created. This is another example of the conservation of matter. The battery is merely the device for changing chemical energy into electrical energy.   J. R. S.
SEE ALSO: BATTERY, CHEMICAL CHANGE, ELECTROLYSIS

Volta's experiment

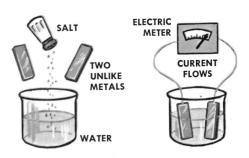

SALT

ELECTRIC METER

TWO UNLIKE METALS

CURRENT FLOWS

WATER

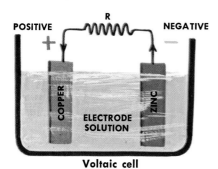

POSITIVE **R** NEGATIVE

COPPER ZINC

ELECTRODE SOLUTION

Voltaic cell

Electrode A conducting surface to which a voltage is applied or at which a voltage is generated is an electrode. In electron tubes, current flows from one electrode to another. In a voltaic cell, two electrodes of different metals dip into a conducting solution. An electromotive force appears between electrodes. In medical instruments, electrodes contact the patient's skin.

Flashlight batteries and storage cells are voltaic cells. The chemical action of the solution in the battery, called an *electrolyte,* creates a potential difference between the electrodes. Different metals have different values of electrode potential. When the two electrodes are connected in a circuit, the potential difference of the electrodes causes current to flow through the circuit from one electrode to another. The electrode which is oxidized in the cell is the *anode* (outside terminal is negative). The other, reducer electrode is the *cathode* (positive terminal).

The flashlight BATTERY, or *dry cell,* contains a carbon rod which is the anode; and the outer covering, generally made of zinc, supplies the cathode or negative terminal. When the switch is turned on, current flows through the bulb from the negative terminal to the positive terminal. Light is created at the expense of the electrical energy of the cell.

In the automobile storage battery, or *wet cell,* the electrodes consist of lead plates. Although both the anode and the cathode are made of lead, their chemical composition is different. The cathode is *lead oxide,* and the anode is a material called *sponge lead.* This type of battery supplies a much larger current than does the dry cell because of the increase in electrode potential.

The dry cell is called a *primary cell* because after continued use the zinc electrode wears out. The lead-oxide cell is called a *secondary cell* because the electrodes can be restored to their original condition by "recharging" the battery. An outside current source is hooked to the electrodes so that the current flows in an opposite direction to that supplied by the battery itself. A. E. L.

SEE ALSO: ANODE, CATHODE, ELECTROLYSIS, ELECTROPLATING

Electroencephalograph (ih-leck-tro-enn-SEFF-uh-loh-graff) There is always electrical activity in the nervous tissue of the BRAIN. An electroencephalograph is a machine which records that electrical activity. The machine is a special device which records changes in electrical potential or voltage. The device amplifies the potential and records it in wave-like tracings called *electroencephalograms.*

The electroencephalograph (EEG) is a VACUUM TUBE device with very sensitive writing pens attached. A very slight change in potential moves the pen up and down on the recording paper.

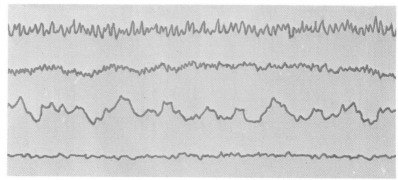

Alpha rhythm: 8-13 per second; normal relaxed adult

Beta rhythm: 13-30 per second; aroused anxious person

Delta rhythm: ½-3 per second; normal, asleep, dreaming

Theta rhythm: 4-7 per second; emotional adolescent

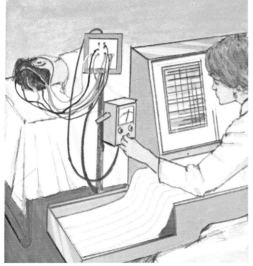

Electrodes placed on the scalp transmit electrical impulses from the brain to the EEG machine.

To use EEG the technician first applies painless ELECTRODES to the patient's scalp with special conductive paste. The end of each electrode is plugged into a junction box that has 16 or more connections or terminals. Each connection is carefully labeled to mark the position of its electrode on the scalp, so that tracings can be associated with that portion of the brain which produced it. The electrodes are conductors through which current passes from the brain to the writing pens, which then trace out the electroencephalograms.

The tracings of the electrical potential of the brain in most human subjects are seen in a reduced or decreased form. This is because the recordings are made from the scalp through the skull, rather than directly from the brain. Direct recordings are mainly obtained with experimental animals.

Measuring the electric potential of the brain furnishes physiological information to medical science. In addition, electroencephalograms are used in diagnosing mental disorders and in detecting organic abnormalities.

Epileptic seizures are outward signs of severe disturbance in electrical activity within the central NERVOUS SYSTEM. Where normal persons show a wave frequency pattern of 8–12 peaks per second, epileptic victims can measure as high as 15–40 spike-like waves per second during an attack; at other times their frequency pattern would be less, but above the normal reading.

In the detection of cerebral tumors, the electroencephalogram shows waves occurring at a lower-than-normal frequency in the region of the scalp overlying the affected area. D. L. D.

SEE ALSO: EPILEPSY

Electrolysis (ih-leck-TRAHL-uh-siss) Many molecules in a solution or a fluid state tend to be easily separated into positive and negative particles or groups, called *ions*. When positive and negative electrical charges are placed at two different points within the fluid, the positive ions migrate to the negative charge and the negative ions go to the positive charge. Thus each ion neutralizes some of the charge placed in the fluid. The ions then recombine with opposite ions to form new molecules. This is called *electrolysis*.

The electrolysis of chemicals is a very important industrial process. There are many substances which cannot be produced economically any other way than by electrolytic decomposition. Some of the important chemicals produced by electrolysis are sodium, chlorine (the process for producing these two elements is discussed below), silver, aluminum, zinc, calcium, fluorine, and many others.

The forces holding a sodium chloride CRYSTAL together are electrical. The sodium has a positive charge and is called a *sodium ion,* and the chlorine has a negative charge and is called a *chloride ion.* An ION is an atom with an electrical charge. This charge results from an atom either losing or gaining electrons. In a tiny crystal containing, say, twelve atoms, the sodium ions attract six chloride ions, and the chloride ions attract the six sodium ions. The crystal is composed of alternating sodium and chloride ions and is called a *crystal lattice.*

These ions are not free to move about until the crystal is melted. When an electric current is passed through the melted salt the ions are attracted to oppositely charged ELECTRODES. The ions carry the electrons by conductance, which is quite different from a current being carried in a wire. A silvery substance (sodium metal) begins to deposit on the negative electrode while a yellow-green gas (chlorine) bubbles off at the positive electrode.

In more detail, each chloride ion that reaches the ANODE (the positive electrode) becomes a neutral chlorine atom by giving up its extra electron to the electrode. It is

✳ **THINGS TO DO**

WHAT SOLUTIONS ARE ELECTROLYTES?

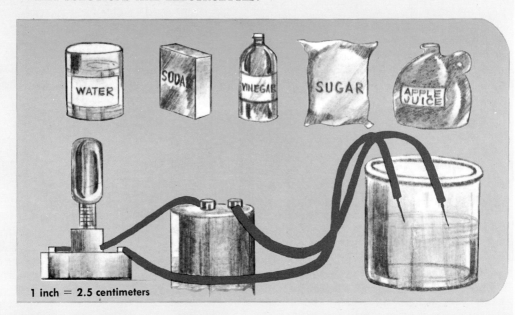

1 inch = 2.5 centimeters

1 Follow the diagram in connecting the dry cell to the light receptacle.
2 Expose three inches of the free ends of the bell wire. These will be placed in glass to test the conductivity of several solutions. If the solution is an electrolyte the bulb will light up.
3 Make a solution with each of these materials: salt, sugar, baking powder, baking soda, vinegar, ink, lemon juice, and apple juice.
4 Test them separately in the circuit arrangement.
5 When certain materials dissolve in water they will dissociate into positive and negatively charged ions. This solution will then conduct an electric current.

possible for two of these atoms then to combine to give the yellow-green gas, chlorine. Similarly the sodium ion accepts an electron from the CATHODE (the negative electrode) to become metallic sodium, the neutral sodium atom. (This reaction should not be confused with the electrolysis of a water solution of sodium chloride.) The following is a chemical equation which summarizes the above discussion:

$$2Na^+ + 2Cl^- \xrightarrow{\text{electricity}} 2Na + Cl_2$$

melted crystals   silvery   green
                       metal   gas

ELECTROPLATING is a rather important result of electrolysis experiments. Electrolysis has been defined as breaking down or decomposing a substance to its elements by an electrical current. In electroplating the principle is the same. Simply, this process is the transference of a metal from one electrode to produce a coating on the other electrode. An easy experiment to perform illustrating the above is to place a piece of shiny zinc in a solution of copper sulfate. The copper will plate out on the zinc. The copper sulfate may be replaced by silver nitrate, rather expensive, to get a silver plate. These plates will not be permanent.

A more recent and extremely important result of electrolysis and ELECTROCHEMISTRY is the *fuel cell*. Even though the fuel cell has been known for many years it has only recently become an important source of electricity. A fuel cell generates electricity without using heat engines or great water sources to run huge *dynamos*. In one sense it is a small chemical electric cell.   J. R. S.

Electrolyte see Battery, Electrolysis, Electroplating

Electromagnet An electromagnet consists of a soft-iron core around which a number of turns of insulated wire are wound. This becomes a MAGNET when connected to a source of ELECTRICITY. When disconnected, it is no longer a magnet.

When the ends of the wire are connected to a source of direct current, such as a BATTERY, the current flowing through the wire creates a *magnetic field*. The function of the iron core in the coil is to further increase the strength or density of the magnetic field. Thus, even though the core is not a magnet itself, it acts as a magnet to increase the strength of the field surrounding the coil.

One advantage of an electromagnet over a permanent magnet is that the strength of the field can be changed at will. If the strength of the magnet is to be increased, the number of turns of wire on the core can be increased, or the amount of current flowing through the coil can be increased. To decrease the strength of the magnet one merely reduces the amount of current or the number of turns of wire in the coil.

Another advantage, probably more important than the first, is that the coil may be magnetized and demagnetized at the will of the operator by merely turning off the supply of direct current. The current stops flowing immediately when the power is shut off, but the iron core still retains a very small amount of magnetization.

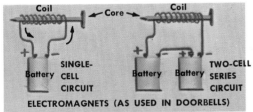

ELECTROMAGNETS (AS USED IN DOORBELLS)

THE HENRY MAGNET 1831

The additional current going through the two-cell circuit will make that one a stronger electromagnet

The original electromagnet made by Joseph Henry is in the Smithsonian Institution

Smithsonian Institution

✳ **THINGS TO DO**

MAKING A HORSESHOE ELECTRO-MAGNET

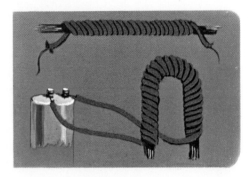

1   Cut several lengths of wire from clothes hangers.
2   Wrap many turns of bell wire around a bundle of the wire pieces, making sure you wrap in one direction.
3   Remove the insulation from the two ends of the bell wire in order to make direct contact with the two terminals of a dry cell. Bend the bundle into a horseshoe shape.
4   Experiment with the magnet when the electric circuit is complete. What materials will the electromagnet pick up?
5   Test the poles with a compass to determine the north and south seeking poles.

The property of retaining a small amount of magnetization, exhibited by most ferrous (iron) metals, is known as *hysteresis*. When the current is first turned on, the field density builds up very rapidly. However, when the current is turned off, the field does not decrease at as rapid a rate as the current. Hence, even though there is no current flowing, there is still some magnetic field present. Reverse current is sometimes used to "kill" the magnetic field.

The electromagnet has many practical uses in everyday living. The doorbell, the telephone and the telegraph all employ electromagnets in some form. Scientists use large electromagnets to study the properties of various materials. The surgeon may use an electromagnet to remove a piece of metal from an injured eye. GENERATORS and electric motors use electromagnets to convert electrical energy to mechanical energy. A.E.L.
SEE ALSO: HENRY, JOSEPH; SOLENOID

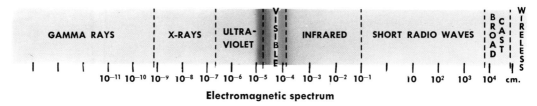

| GAMMA RAYS | X-RAYS | ULTRA-VIOLET | VISIBLE | INFRARED | SHORT RADIO WAVES | BROADCAST | WIRELESS |

10^{-11} 10^{-10} 10^{-9} 10^{-8} 10^{-7} 10^{-6} 10^{-5} 10^{-4} 10^{-3} 10^{-2} 10^{-1} 10 10^2 10^3 10^4 cm.

Electromagnetic spectrum

Electromagnetic spectrum Just as the ear has certain limits in hearing sound, the eye has limits in detecting light. There are both upper and lower limits in each case. The eye cannot see electromagnetic radiation beyond the violet region of the SPECTRUM and below the red region. The ranges above and below these limits, including the visible range, make up the *electromagnetic spectrum*. Even though the last wave length considered in the visible range is 4×10^{-5} cm (0.0016 inch), some persons can detect radiation with a wave length as small as 3×10^{-5} cm (0.00012 inch).

Radiation which has a wave length shorter than 4×10^{-5} cm is called *ultraviolet light*. This region extends down to a wave length of about 5×10^{-7} cm. Still lower than this region is the region of X-RAYS which extends to a wave length of about 6×10^{-10} cm. The lowest end of the spectrum is made up of waves called *"gamma rays."* This extends down from the X ray region.

On the side of the longer light wave, that is beyond the red, lies the region called *infrared*. This extends from 7×10^{-5} to 4×10^{-2} cm. Next comes the region of microwaves, have wave lengths 4×10^{-2} to 10^2 cm. Beyond this come three bands of RADIO waves: shortwave, 10^2 to 10^4 cm; broadcast band, 2×10^4 to 6×10^4 cm; long radio waves, greater than 6×10^4 cm.

It is interesting to note that only a very small region of the spectrum contains radiation which can be detected by the eye. Even though the waves in different regions all have the same properties, the term *light* is assigned only to the visible portion of the spectrum and the two areas adjoining it.

The visible light portions of the spectrum are emitted by hot bodies. The gamma ray region are the result of radioactive decay. Radio waves can be generated by electrical discharges. Although definite lines are shown separating the different regions, there is no real distinct separation.   A. E. L.

SEE ALSO: LIGHT; RAY, GAMMA; RAY, ULTRA-VIOLET; SOUND

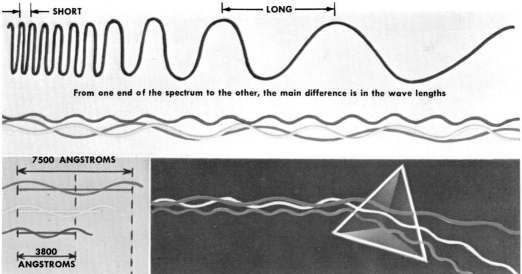

From one end of the spectrum to the other, the main difference is in the wave lengths

7500 ANGSTROMS

3800 ANGSTROMS

Visible light is part of the electromagnetic spectrum with wave lengths between 3800 angstroms and 7500 angstroms. Red waves are about twice as long as violet waves

Electromotive force Electromotive force (EMF) is the electric pressure caused by a difference in potential between the terminals of a device used to supply current. It causes ELECTRICITY to flow in a circuit.

Electron An electron is a subatomic particle of matter. It has a small, negative electric charge, a very small mass, and is extremely small in size. Electric currents are attributed to the movement of electrons.

The electron is visualized as revolving in specific orbits around the *nucleus* of the atom. Although recent experiments have shown that this is not entirely correct, the model is still useful in understanding the actions of electrons. Chemists refer to these orbits as *shells*. The *valence* of a particular element depends on the number of electrons present in the outermost shell of a given atom. The rapidly moving electrons striking a metal target are responsible for the emission of X RAYS from the metal.

Experimental evidence has further shown that in addition to revolving around the nucleus, an electron is also spinning around its own axis. This is a situation very similar to the earth revolving around the sun. The spin of electrons is responsible for the magnetic properties of certain elements such as iron.

Scientists have discovered that the electron also has a counterpart which has been called a *positron*. It has the same mass as an electron but the electric charge is positive rather than negative. Positrons (positive electrons) exist only for very short periods of time and are not part of ordinary matter.   A. E. L.

SEE ALSO: BOHR THEORY, COMPOUND, ELECTRICITY, ELECTRON BORROWING, ELEMENTS, ELECTRONICS, MILLIKAN'S ELECTRONIC CHARGE, RUTHERFORD THEORY, X RAYS

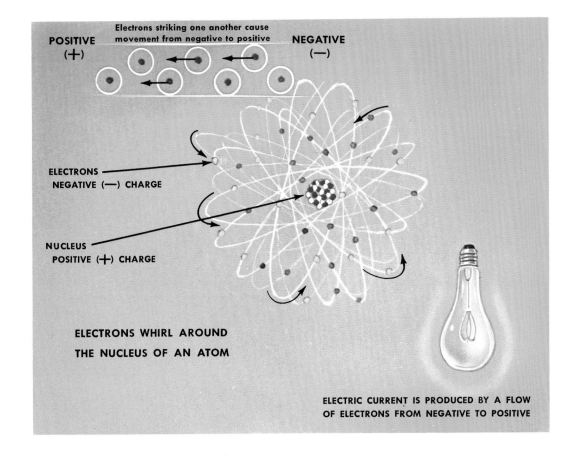

POSITIVE (+)   Electrons striking one another cause movement from negative to positive   NEGATIVE (−)

ELECTRONS NEGATIVE (−) CHARGE

NUCLEUS POSITIVE (+) CHARGE

ELECTRONS WHIRL AROUND THE NUCLEUS OF AN ATOM

ELECTRIC CURRENT IS PRODUCED BY A FLOW OF ELECTRONS FROM NEGATIVE TO POSITIVE

Electron borrowing Atoms that are alike combine to form ELEMENTS, such as gold, silver, oxygen, mercury. Atoms that are different combine to form COMPOUNDS, such as salt or water. In nature, only a few pure elements are found. Most matter is made up of compounds. Some of these combinations are strong and it is hard to separate the atoms; others are weak and separation is easier. The forces that hold the atoms together are electrical. It is the little charges of negative electricity, electrons, that determine how different atoms will combine to form molecules of compounds.

Each ATOM contains a center, or nucleus, surrounded by whirling electrons. The atom itself is electrically neutral because its nucleus has a positive charge which is exactly balanced by an equal number of negatively charged electrons. Atoms of the same elements have the same number of electrons. Atoms of different elements have a different number of electrons.

Electrons seem to orbit around their nuclei in shells, each shell capable of holding a definite number of electrons. The innermost shell can hold two electrons: the next, eight; the next, eighteen; etc. Gold, for instance, has electrons in shells 2-8-18-32-18-1, seventy-nine in all. The number of electrons in an atom, and particularly the number in the outer shell, determines how different kinds of atoms will combine. Some atoms will easily give up one or more of their electrons to a nearby atom to form different compounds. The atom that gives up its electron thus has an excess of protons and becomes a *positive ion*. The atom that accepts or borrows the electron now has an excess of electrons and becomes a *negative ion*. Compounds formed by transfer of electrons from one atom to another are said to be *electrovalent*. In general, water solutions of electrovalent compounds are good *electrolytes*.

An example of ELECTRON borrowing is the common compound salt, which is made up of sodium and chlorine.   H. W. M.

SEE ALSO: COMPOUNDS, STABILITY OF; ELECTROLYTE; ION

Electron microscope see Biophysics; Microscope, electron

Electron sharing Some atoms combine by sharing electrons instead of borrowing them. This makes a strong combination that is hard to break up.

A very simple example is the combination of two hydrogen atoms to form a molecule of hydrogen. Each hydrogen atom contains

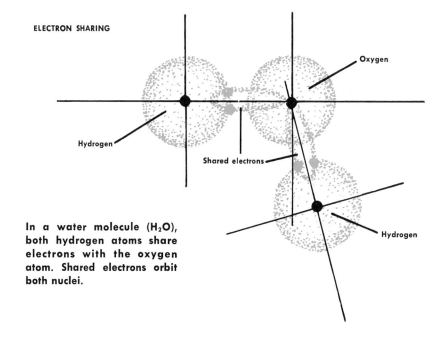

ELECTRON SHARING

Oxygen

Hydrogen

Shared electrons

Hydrogen

In a water molecule (H₂O), both hydrogen atoms share electrons with the oxygen atom. Shared electrons orbit both nuclei.

one electron. In combination, both electrons orbit around both nuclei, each thereby sharing a second electron.

COMPOUNDS which are formed by sharing electrons are called *covalent compounds.* Compounds of carbon (*organic* compounds) are generally formed by electron sharing. In this process no transfer of electrons occurs. *Methane* is one of the simpler carbon compounds so formed. Its four hydrogen atoms each share one of their electrons with one carbon atom so that all the atoms have their quota of electrons in the outer shell.

SEE ALSO: ELECTRON BORROWING

Electron tube see Electronics

Electronic music see Musical instruments

Electronics Electronics is the branch of science and engineering relating to the motion and control of electrons. Electronics is related to the science of ELECTRICITY. Both involve the study of *electric current.* However, the two fields differ in their viewpoints. Electricity focuses on the use and transfer of electric current in the form of energy. This energy operates electric lights, appliances, and other equipment. Electronics involves the use of electronic devices that convert electric current into signals or pulses. These signals supply information, such as sound, pictures, or numbers, and are used in TV sets, radios, computers, and other equipment. In the past, the most commonly used electronic devices were *vacuum tubes.* Today, these have mostly been replaced by *solid state devices* such as transistors and semiconductor diodes.

BASIC ELECTRONIC FUNCTIONS

To understand how electronic devices work, it is important to understand the nature of electric current. All matter is made up of ATOMS, which are in turn made up of smaller particles. One of these particles is the negatively charged ELECTRON. Electrons are

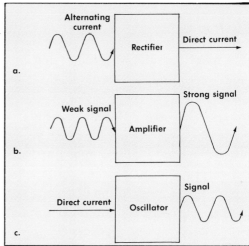

Electronic devices change the way current flows. (a) A rectifier converts alternating current to direct current. (b) An amplifier changes a weak signal into a stronger signal. (c) An oscillator converts direct current into a signal.

attracted to positive charges and repelled by other negative charges. When electrons move as a result of their repulsion or attraction to other charges, they form an electric current.

Electronic devices change the way current flows. Most devices can change the current flow in one of four ways: through *rectification,* through *amplification,* through *oscillation,* or through *switching.* By combining these functions in various ways, engineers can create electronic equipment such as computers, televisions, and stereos.

Rectification is the simplest and most basic electronic operation. Devices that perform rectification are called *rectifiers.* Rectifiers convert *alternating current* to *direct current.* This forces the current to flow in only one direction instead of allowing it to flow in both directions. Most electronic equipment today uses *semiconductor diodes* as rectifiers. Older equipment uses *vacuum tubes.*

Amplification is the process of strengthening a weak signal to produce a stronger signal. This function is performed by devices called *amplifiers.* Today, *transistors* are used as amplifiers, but in the past vacuum tubes provided this function.

Oscillation changes direct current into a signal. The devices that perform oscillation are called *oscillators.* These devices are actually forms of amplifiers—they strengthen a signal and then combine it with the original signal to produce a new signal with a different frequency. Transistors are common oscillators in modern equipment.

Switching is the process of turning on and off electric circuits. This operation is usually performed by transistors.

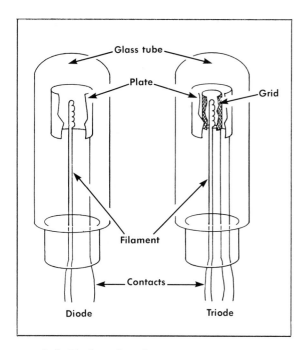

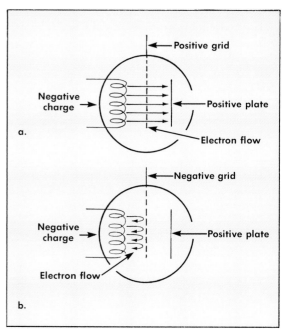

Left: Diode and triode vacuum tubes. Right: The grid in a triode controls the current flow to the plate. (a) If the grid is positive, it attracts electrons and current reaches the plate. (b) If the grid is negative, it repels electrons and current does not reach the plate.

VACUUM TUBES

Vacuum tubes are part of a larger family of devices known as *electron tubes*. These devices were used extensively during the first half of the twentieth century.

A vacuum tube is a glass tube from which almost all of the air has been pumped out. Various metallic elements in the tube produce and control a beam of electrons.

There are several types of vacuum tubes. The simplest type is known as a *diode*. In a diode, one end of a tube contains a filament, and the other end often contains a metal plate. When the filament is heated, it releases a stream of electrons that move through the tube. When the plate is given a positive charge, the electrons move in a stream toward the plate. But if the plate is given a negative charge, the electrons are repelled and no current flows. Because diodes force the current to flow in a single direction, they can be used as *rectifiers*.

A *triode* is a slightly more complicated form of vacuum tube. A triode is basically a diode with a spiral piece of wire inserted between the filament and the plate. This wire is called a *grid*. The grid is given a negative charge. By changing the amount of negative charge on the grid, the current flow

to the plate can be increased or decreased, thus creating an *amplifier*. When a triode amplifier is arranged so that some of the current to the plate is "fed back" to the grid, an *oscillator* is formed.

Although vacuum tubes are very versatile, they have several disadvantages: they are large, they require a source of power to heat the filaments, and they usually wear out after several thousand hours of use. Today, only a few specialty vacuum tubes, such as microwave tubes and CATHODE-RAY TUBES, are used in electronic devices.

A cathode ray tube

SOLID STATE DEVICES

In a *solid state device,* electrons flow through certain solid materials instead of through a vacuum. The materials used in solid state devices are generally grouped into three classes: *insulators,* which prevent the flow of electrons; *conductors,* which allow the passage of the electrons; and *semiconductors,* which can be treated to form insulators or conductors. Most solid state devices are made from semiconductors.

Semiconductors are crystals with a nearly perfect structure. Certain impurities can be added to a semiconductor so that it has an excess of free electrons. This form of semiconductor is known as an *n-semiconductor.* Other impurities produce *p-semiconductors,* which have a deficiency of free electrons. By combining the two forms of semiconductors in different ways, different electronic devices can be created.

A *semiconductor diode* is formed when a layer of n-type silicon is placed next to a layer of p-type silicon. The boundary between the two layers is known as a *pn junction.* Electrons flow in one direction from the negatively charged n-layer to the positively charged p-layer.

A *transistor* contains three layers of semiconducting material. One type of transistor is the *npn transistor,* which contains a layer of p-type material "sandwiched" between two layers of n-type material. Another type of transistor is the *pnp transistor,* which contains a layer of n-type material "sandwiched" between two layers of p-type material.

In both types of transistors, the outside layers are known as the *emitter* and *collector,* while the middle layer is called the *base.* The functions of these layers are roughly similar to the functions of the filament, plate, and grid of the triode vacuum tube. Thus, the arrangement of material in a transistor allows it to act as an amplifier, oscillator, or switch.

Some solid state devices also serve as sources and sensors of light and radiation. *Light-emitting diodes* are semiconductor devices that form the lighted displays on many computers and watches. *Lasers* use crystals, such as rubies, to amplify light. The light beam produced by a laser can be so strong it can burn holes through extremely hard substances, or it can be controlled so that it barely affects the surface of the skin.

Other solid state devices include *superconductors,* which can carry an intense electric current, and *cryotrons,* which are used as switches in computers and other electronic equipment.

ELECTRONIC CIRCUITS

In electronic equipment, electronic devices are connected together to form an electronic circuit. The components and their connections form a complete path through which the electric current flows.

Until the late 1950s, most circuits were made up of separate components that were joined by wires or other conductors. These circuits, known as *conventional circuits,* tended to be large and cumbersome. As they became

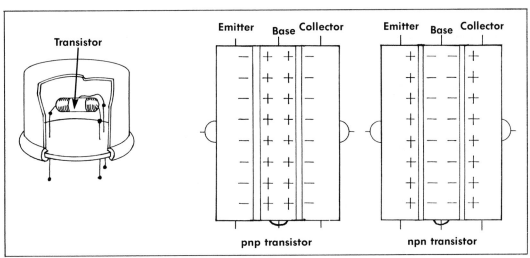

A transistor consists of three layers of semiconducting materials. A pnp transistor has a layer of n-type material between two layers of p-type materials. An npn transistor has a layer of p-type material between two layers of n-type material.

more complicated, the wiring process took more time.

During the 1960s, a new process for creating circuits was developed. This process involves chemically altering a piece of silicon so that it can conduct current in different ways. By altering the behavior of the silicon, engineers can produce rectifiers, amplifiers, oscillators, and switches all on a tiny piece of material. This type of circuit is called an *integrated circuit,* and is used in devices such as watches, computers, televisions, and even automobiles.

MAKING INTEGRATED CIRCUITS

Making integrated circuits involves several key steps. The silicon used for the circuits is extracted from common rocks and sand. It is then melted down in a form that is 99.9 percent pure silicon and "grown" into cylindrical crystals. These cylindrical crystals are sliced into thin wafers about 1/250 of an inch

(0.1 millimeter) thick. Each wafer will eventually hold hundreds of integrated circuits.

The surfaces of the wafers are then sterilized and polished to a mirrorlike finish. Then they are coated with a silicon-dioxide film, which is created by placing the wafers in an open glass tube and placing it in an oxidation furnace. Oxygen reacts with the silicon, creating a thin layer of silicon dioxide. Next, the wafers are coated with a gelatin-like substance called *photoresist,* which is a light-sensitive material. Stencils for the circuit pattern are placed on top of the photoresist and the wafers are exposed to ultraviolet light. The light hardens the photoresist, except for areas that are covered by the stencil.

Acids and solvents are used to remove the areas of the photoresist that are still soft. The silicon dioxide that is exposed by the washing process is etched away with hot gases so that pathways of pure silicon run through the layer of hardened photoresist.

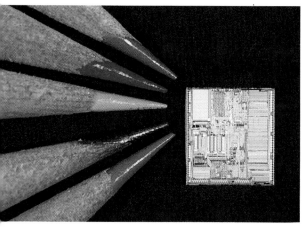

A single integrated circuit microprocessor "chip" (top left) is surprisingly tiny. Several chips are laid out on a circuit board to run a computer (bottom left). Another solid state device, a laser diode (top right), emits a laser beam that operates laser disc (bottom right) and compact disc players. (All photos © Cameramann Intl., Ltd.)

At this point impurities are added to the silicon in a process called *doping*. These impurities form positive and negative conducting zones.

The steps for treating the wafers are repeated several times, using a different stencil each time. This builds up layers on the wafers. After all the layers have been created, aluminum is deposited on the wafer to fill in gaps and connect the circuit components. Finally, the circuits are tested. Those that pass the testing are cut from the wafers to be packaged and used. M.K.H.

SEE ALSO: ATOM, ELECTRICITY, ELECTRON, ENERGY, LASER, PHOTOELECTRICITY, RADAR, RADIO, SEMICONDUCTOR, SUPERCONDUCTOR, TELEVISION, TRANSISTOR, VACUUM TUBE

Electroplating Electroplating is the process of putting a thin, protective layer of metal on the surface of other metals. The metals would rust in the open air if they were not electroplated. It may also be used to decorate metal and to repair certain items.

It is necessary to clean the surface of the item to be plated. All oil or grease must be removed. All roughness must be smoothed away. This is done by using an ABRASIVE wheel or a metal scratch brush. The metal is then cleaned in a soap or alkali bath followed by a clean water rinse. Rust particles and scales can be removed by dipping the metal into a pickling acid.

When the item is smooth and clean, it is ready to be placed in the electrolyte bath. This bath is a solution of some SALT of the metal to be used in plating and other salts, acids or alkalies which increase the conductivity of the solution. This increase makes it possible to plate with a minimum amount of current in the shortest time. An ANODE and a CATHODE are placed at opposite ends of a tank which contains the electrolyte. The item to be plated is the cathode and the supply of metal for coating is the anode. As the current passes through the electrolyte, the metal of the anode dissolves and positive ions of the metal deposit on the cathode. D. E. Z.

SEE ALSO: ELECTROLYSIS

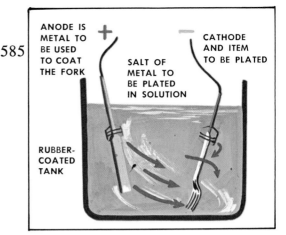

ANODE IS METAL TO BE USED TO COAT THE FORK

SALT OF METAL TO BE PLATED IN SOLUTION

CATHODE AND ITEM TO BE PLATED

RUBBER-COATED TANK

Metallic ions from the anode are deposited as a coating on the cathode

Electroscope An electroscope detects small charges or currents of ELECTRICITY, and tells whether the charges are negative or positive. Some measure the voltage of small charges.

Electrostatic precipitator An electrostatic precipitator is used to remove small particles and dust from smoke that causes air pollution.

The electrostatic precipitator removes the particles by using *direct current*. Large plates inside the precipitator are charged with electricity. The plates cause the particles to become charged. The charged particles are then attached to a plate of opposite charge and removed from the smoke. The plates become covered with particles. When the plates are covered, the electricity is turned off, and the particles fall off. A.J.H.

Electrostatics Electrostatics is the study of static electricity. Static electricity is charge at rest. Electrostatics deals with how static charges are produced and the electrostatic forces of attraction and repulsion.

Early Greek philosophers were the first to study electrostatics. Thales studied static electricity about 600 B.C. The Greeks found that amber, when rubbed with cloth, attracted bits of straw and leaves.

CHARLES COULOMB established a mathematical relationship that connected force of attraction, charge, and distance between charges.

Today the Van de Graff generator, an electrostatic device, is used to accelerate particles for nuclear study. A.J.H.

SEE ALSO: ACCELERATOR

Elements All matter is made up of tiny particles. These particles are so small that they must be magnified many million times in order to be seen. These tiny particles are called ATOMS. An element is made up of atoms of one single type.

The number of different elements is rather small when one notices the thousands of different kinds of matter in the world. There are only 105 elements known at this time, and most are rare. Some elements are not found in nature, but are made by man in special laboratories, and under very special conditions. There are only a few elements that might be called common and plentiful.

ROBERT BOYLE, the English scientist, proposed the first definition of an element that is still valuable today. He felt there were certain substances that could not be broken down into simpler substances. These substances were called *elements*. One reason his definition has withstood the test of time and experiment is that it is an operational definition. Many substances were thought to be elements since there was no method, at that time, to break them down further. As methods and techniques improved, more and more substances were broken down into smaller parts. Some substances have resisted all attempts to decompose them. These substances are elements.

To define an element precisely in simple terms is extraordinarily difficult. Without knowledge of modern physics it would be proper to say "An element is a substance that cannot be broken down or decomposed into smaller parts by ordinary chemical means." There are elements that change into other elements by RADIOACTIVITY. This is not classified as true chemical change. On this basis there are 105 elements, not counting ISOTOPES but including man-made elements. Of these, 18 elements (and many isotopes) are radioactive.

ARCHITECTURE OF THE ELEMENTS

Since the elements are made up of many atoms, the architecture, or structure, of the elements is dependent upon the architecture of the atoms.

All elements are made up of the same basic material: PROTONS, positively-charged particles, and ELECTRONS, negatively-charged particles. There are also NEUTRONS which have no charge.

An element is a kind of matter all of which has atoms with the same number of protons. This number is referred to as the *atomic number*. Generally what makes one element different from another is nothing more than the specific number of protons.

The protons are found in the center of the atom, called the *nucleus*. The neutrons are found there also. The space they occupy is extremely small. The electrons are found circling outside the nucleus. The same number of electrons would be associated with an atom as there are protons. A positive charge neutralizes a negative charge; thus, an atom is electrically neutral.

HYDROGEN, the first element, has a single proton in the nucleus and one electron outside the nucleus. There are two other forms of hydrogen, both very rare. They are called ISOTOPES of hydrogen. In addition to the proton there is a neutron in the nucleus which does not change the chemical properties to any great extent. This form of hydrogen is called DEUTERIUM. The third form is radioactive and called *tritium*. It has the one proton, but, in addition, two neutrons in the nucleus. There is only one electron circling these nuclei as in the first case.

The three forms of hydrogen are different only in the number of neutrons in the nucleus

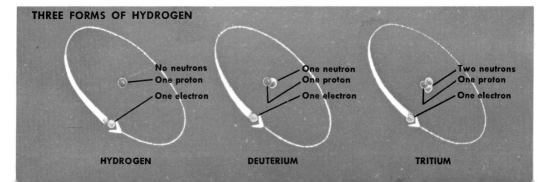

THREE FORMS OF HYDROGEN

No neutrons
One proton
One electron

One neutron
One proton
One electron

Two neutrons
One proton
One electron

HYDROGEN   DEUTERIUM   TRITIUM

Elements

The atoms of different elements build up in a progressive manner, adding protons and neutrons to the nucleus and electrons to the outer portions.

NAMES AND SYMBOLS

Some elements which are quite familiar are silver, gold, iron, copper, aluminum, sulfur, oxygen, and carbon. Abbreviations—symbols—for these and the names of the other elements are usually the initial letter of the name plus an additional letter when necessary—Al for aluminum, S for sulfur, O for oxygen, and C for carbon. In some cases the initial letters of the Latin or Greek are used: Ag for silver (*argentum*), Au for gold (*aurum*), Fe for iron (*ferrum*), and Cu for copper (*cuprum*).

PERIODIC TABLE

Mendeleev, and Meyer independently, found that if the elements were arranged in the order of their ascending atomic weights, the chemical properties change from one element to the next in a definite way, but they return to about the same value at fixed points in the series. Mendeleev drew up a table in which the elements were arranged in horizontal rows called *periods* according to their atomic weights and in vertical columns (*groups* or *families*) according to their similarities. This periodic table was somewhat inaccurate because the atomic weights were not known accurately. Modern tables are based on ascending atomic number, since the atomic number determines the properties of the element. The table on pages 588-589 lists all recognized elements as of 1981 by ascending atomic number.

VALENCE AND BONDING

When elements combine with one another, a chemical change occurs. The elements no longer have the same properties. For example, if the poisonous alkali metal SODIUM is added to the poisonous halogen CHLORINE, the resulting compound is sodium chloride, common table salt.

Valence is a measure of the ability of an atom to combine with other atoms. Hydrogen has the simplest atomic structures; the VALENCE of hydrogen is +1, by definition. The valence of any other element is defined as the number of hydrogen atoms which one atom of that element combines with, or replaces in a COMPOUND. Chlorine, for example, has a valence of −1 because one

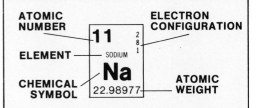

HOW TO READ THE PERIODIC TABLE

All the elements are listed by their *atomic number*. The atomic number is the number of protons in the nucleus of an atom of the element.

The *chemical symbol* for the element can be the first two letters of the element's name, or the first two letters of its Latin or Greek name. (The Latin name for sodium is *natrium.*)

The *atomic weight* of an element is found by comparing its weight to the weight of carbon-12, an *isotope* of carbon.

A single atom of an element has different energy levels surrounding it. (You can imagine these levels as shells that fit one outside another.) In the first energy level of an atom the atom can have 2 electrons; in the second it can have 8; in the third, 18. Sodium has 2 electrons in its first energy level, 8 in its second, but only 1 in its third. When an energy level is not filled, the atom is very reactive, and tends to form compounds to share the electrons in energy levels that are not completely filled. The *electron configuration* tells how many electrons an atom of an element has.

atom of chlorine will combine with one atom of hydrogen to form hydrochloric acid (HCl). Sodium (Na), however, has a valence of +1 because one atom of sodium will replace the hydrogen in the compound HCl, giving NaCl, or table salt.

An element with a valence of +1 will donate one electron to another atom in combining with it. An atom with a valence of −1 will accept one electron in forming a compound. These electrons are usually lost from or gained by the *outer shell* of the atom. When electrons are lost or gained by an atom, the atom becomes charged, or an ION. This is *ionic bonding.*

Many elements do not form ionic bonds because they cannot easily give up or gain electrons. These atoms combine by *sharing* the electrons in their outer shells. This type of bonding is called *covalent bonding.*

All members of a group of elements have the same valence, the same number of electrons in their outer shells.   J. R. S.

SEE ALSO: CHEMISTRY, GAS, INDIVIDUAL ELEMENTS, MENDELEEV'S PERIODIC TABLE, NUCLEAR SCIENCE, RADIATION, SYMBOL

Fisher Scientific

Periodic Cha

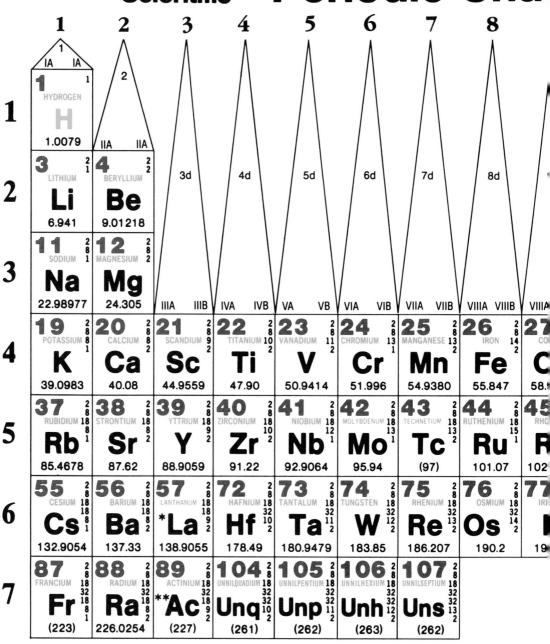

THE SYMBOL. Shown in the middle of each block directly below the name of the element. The color used indicates the physical state of the element under ordinary conditions: black for solids, green for liquids and blue for gases.

THE ATOMIC WEIGHT. Directly below the symbol for each element the atomic weight is shown in black. The values are taken from the official Report on Atomic Weights Cf. J. Amer. Chem. Soc. 84, 4193 (1976). For elements not listed in the Report the mass number of the longest lived isotope is shown in brackets.

THE ATOMIC NUMBER. Shown in red in the upper left hand corner.

ELECTRONIC CONFIGURATION. Shown at the upper right as a group of black numerals. When read downward they indicate the number of electrons normally found in successive energy levels.

EDUCATIONAL MATERIALS DIVISION
4901 W. LeMoyne St.
Chicago, IL 60651
(312) 378-7770

©Copyright 1985

f the Elements

10	11	12	•13	14	15	16	17	18

Periodic table of the elements (right portion)

Group headers: 10, 11, 12, •13, 14, 15, 16, 17, 18

| | 11d | 12d | 13 ◆
■ ★
IIIB IIIA | 14
IVB IVA | 15
VB VA | 16
VIB VIA | 17
VIIB VIIA | 18
0 VIIIA |

18 / 0 / VIIIA column:

2 — HELIUM — **He** — 4.00260 — (2, 2)

| 5 BORON **B** 10.81 (2,3) | 6 CARBON **C** 12.011 (2,4) | 7 NITROGEN **N** 14.0067 (2,5) | 8 OXYGEN **O** 15.9994 (2,6) | 9 FLUORINE **F** 18.998403 (2,7) | 10 NEON **Ne** 20.179 (2,8) |

| 13 ALUMINUM **Al** 26.98154 (2,8,3) | 14 SILICON **Si** 28.0855 (2,8,4) | 15 PHOSPHORUS **P** 30.97376 (2,8,5) | 16 SULPHUR **S** 32.06 (2,8,6) | 17 CHLORINE **Cl** 35.453 (2,8,7) | 18 ARGON **Ar** 39.948 (2,8,8) |

Bottom header row: VIIIB | IB | IB | IIB | IIB

| 29 COPPER **Cu** 63.546 (2,8,18,1) | 30 ZINC **Zn** 65.38 (2,8,18,2) | 31 GALLIUM **Ga** 69.72 (2,8,18,3) | 32 GERMANIUM **Ge** 72.59 (2,8,18,4) | 33 ARSENIC **As** 74.9216 (2,8,18,5) | 34 SELENIUM **Se** 78.96 (2,8,18,6) | 35 BROMINE **Br** 79.904 (2,8,18,7) | 36 KRYPTON **Kr** 83.80 (2,8,18,8) |

(Ni 16,2 ...70)

| 47 SILVER **Ag** 107.868 (2,8,18,18,1) | 48 CADMIUM **Cd** 112.41 (2,8,18,18,2) | 49 INDIUM **In** 114.82 (2,8,18,18,3) | 50 TIN **Sn** 118.69 (2,8,18,18,4) | 51 ANTIMONY **Sb** 121.75 (2,8,18,18,5) | 52 TELLURIUM **Te** 127.60 (2,8,18,18,6) | 53 IODINE **I** 126.9045 (2,8,18,18,7) | 54 XENON **Xe** 131.30 (2,8,18,18,8) |

(...6.4)

| 79 GOLD **Au** 196.9665 (2,8,18,32,18,1) | 80 MERCURY **Hg** 200.59 (2,8,18,32,18,2) | 81 THALLIUM **Tl** 204.37 (2,8,18,32,18,3) | 82 LEAD **Pb** 207.2 (2,8,18,32,18,4) | 83 BISMUTH **Bi** 208.9804 (2,8,18,32,18,5) | 84 POLONIUM **Po** (209) (2,8,18,32,18,6) | 85 ASTATINE **At** (210) (2,8,18,32,18,7) | 86 RADON **Rn** (222) (2,8,18,32,18,8) |

(...t 17,1 / 5.09)

- ● New IUPAC
- ■ Former IUPAC
- ◆ New Chemical Abstract Service
- ★ Former Chemical Abstract Service

| 64 GADOLINIUM **Gd** 157.25 (2,8,18,25,9,2) | 65 TERBIUM **Tb** 158.9254 (2,8,18,26,9,2) | 66 DYSPROSIUM **Dy** 162.50 (2,8,18,28,8,2) | 67 HOLMIUM **Ho** 164.9304 (2,8,18,29,8,2) | 68 ERBIUM **Er** 167.26 (2,8,18,30,8,2) | 69 THULIUM **Tm** 168.9342 (2,8,18,31,8,2) | 70 YTTERBIUM **Yb** 173.04 (2,8,18,32,8,2) | 71 LUTECIUM **Lu** 174.97 (2,8,18,32,9,2) |

(...u .96)

| 96 CURIUM **Cm** (247) (2,8,18,32,25,9,2) | 97 BERKELIUM **Bk** (247) | 98 CALIFORNIUM **Cf** (251) | 99 EINSTEINIUM **Es** (254) | 100 FERMIUM **Fm** (257) | 101 MENDELEVIUM **Md** (258) | 102 NOBELIUM **No** (259) | 103 LAWRENCIUM **Lr** (260) |

(...m 25,8,2 / 43)

Cat. No. S45520

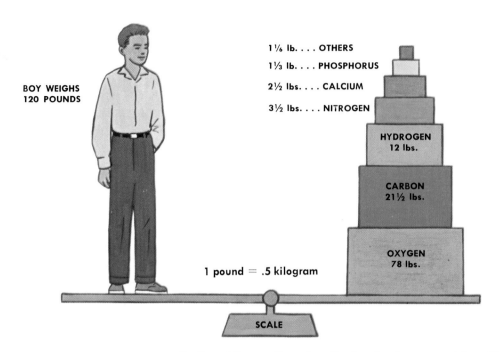

BOY WEIGHS
120 POUNDS

1 ⅙ lb. . . . OTHERS
1 ⅓ lb. . . . PHOSPHORUS
2 ½ lbs. . . . CALCIUM
3 ½ lbs. . . . NITROGEN

HYDROGEN
12 lbs.

CARBON
21 ½ lbs.

OXYGEN
78 lbs.

1 pound = .5 kilogram

SCALE

Elements in the human body All things are made of only a very few, simple materials called chemical ELEMENTS. These elements may be thought of as the simplest kind of building blocks which can be used to make all things. Scientists today know of 92 natural elements, or building blocks, in the world. Most of the human body is made of only six basic building blocks, with small amounts of 14 to 18 other elements.

The human body is about 72 per cent water and only 28 per cent other materials. By weight, the body of an average 120-pound (54.43-kilogram) boy or girl would contain the following weights of the different elements: 78 pounds (35.38 kilograms) of OXYGEN, the invisible gas in air that keeps fires burning; 21½ pounds (9.75 kilograms) of CARBON, the black powder on burnt toast or in a piece of coal; and 12 pounds (5.44 kilograms) of HYDROGEN, a gas used to fill balloons to make them rise. Such a body would also contain 3½ pounds (1.58 kilograms) of NITROGEN, the gas that makes up four-fifths of the air; 2½ pounds (1.13 kilograms) of CALCIUM, a white, silvery element found in lime; and 1⅓ pounds (.6 kilogram) of PHOSPHORUS, the red powder

found on the heads of some matches. These six elements would make up nearly 119 pounds (53.97 kilograms) of the weight of a 120-pound (54.43-kilogram) boy or girl. The other 1⅙ pound (.53 kilogram) consists of small amounts of about 14 other elements, including the metals aluminum, cobalt, zinc, copper, manganese, magnesium, potassium, iron, and sodium; and some of the non-metals, such as sulfur, chlorine, iodine, fluorine, and silicon.

The body obtains these necessary materials from foods. In order to receive enough of these basic building blocks of the body, one must eat sufficient amounts of at least four basic foods: carbohydrates, fats, proteins and minerals. Carbohydrates, fats and proteins supply carbon, hydrogen, oxygen, and some nitrogen, sulfur, and phosphorus. Other elements are derived from minerals, salts, and water.

The human body is a delicately-balanced chemical machine. The body is composed of the above elements grouped in hundreds of different combinations called *chemical compounds*. These elements are the raw materials needed to keep the body in good health. If the body is long deprived of any one or more of these, disease or death will soon result.   R. S. C.

SEE ALSO: CARBOHYDRATES, COMPOUND, FAT, ORGANIC COMPOUNDS, PROTEIN, VITAMINS

Courtesy Society For Visual Education, Inc.
African elephant

Chicago Natural History Museum
Indian elephant

Elephant The elephant is the largest of land animals. Although elephants are not found wild in North America, they are seen in zoos and circuses. They are fascinating to young and old from their peculiar trunks to the tip of their slender tails. Their bodies are covered with thick gray hide with hairs an inch (2.54 centimeters) apart. Elephant skin is wrinkled and looks as if it were too large.

An elephant's trunk is a wonderful tool. It may be 6 feet (1.83 meters) long and weigh 200 to 300 pounds (90.72 to 136.08 kilograms). He can push over a small tree with it and then pick up the smallest leaf. An elephant is a plant eater and eats 200 to 300 pounds (90.72 to 136.08 kilograms) of food a day. An elephant has a pair of highly developed upper teeth called *tusks*. They may be used for fighting.

Overall, an elephant may stand 11 feet (3.35 meters) high and weigh six tons, or 12,000 pounds (5443.1 kilograms). Its huge ears are keen, but it has poor eyesight.

Cow, or female, elephants give birth to one calf at a time after a gestation period of twenty-one to twenty-two months. The young elephant is weaned at two or three years of age, can bear young at fourteen or fifteen, and has a life span similar to that of a man—sixty to eighty years.

There are only two kinds of elephants, the African and the Asiatic, or Indian elephant as it is commonly called. J. K. K.
SEE ALSO: ANIMALS, LIFE SPAN; GESTATION PERIOD

Elephantiasis see Filaria

Elimination see Excretory system

Elk see Deer family

	AFRICAN	INDIAN
HEIGHT	Taller. Shoulder is highest point	Back is highest point
WEIGHT	Heavier	Bulkier but slightly lighter
HEAD	More rounded forehead	Flatter with ridge in center
EARS	Larger	Smaller
TUSKS	Larger	Smaller
TRUNK	Two finger—like knob at end	One finger—like knob at end
COLOR	Darker gray	Gray
HIDE	Rougher	Smoother
USE	Heavy labor, fewer domesticated	Zoos, circuses, heavy labor. Easily domesticated

Elm tree, leaf and fruit

Elm The elm is an important hard-wood tree. The simple leaves have jagged edges. Red or greenish flowers hang in clusters. They develop into a flying fruit *(samara)* which is dry and has one seed.

The fountain-shaped *American elm* can be identified by the secondary trunks, which fork out halfway up, and the leafy top, which gives it a fan-shaped appearance. This majestic shade tree of so many towns and cities is fast disappearing. The *Dutch elm disease* was introduced in the United States in 1930. Since then, the small bark beetle has carried the fungus across the country, destroying thousands of trees.

The *rock* or *cork elm* has fine decorative wood so strong and durable it is used to make wheel spokes, sturdy furniture, railway ties and ship parts.

The *slippery elm* gets its name from the fact that a mucilage in the bark used to be extracted and used to soothe sore throats. It has rough leaves and bark.   H.J.C.

Embalm (emm-BAHM) To embalm is to treat a dead body in such a way as to preserve it from decay. This used to be done using spices and drugs. It is now done by removing the blood and injecting a fluid containing for-maldehyde, alcohol, salts and dyes. Embalming is practiced to preserve a body prior to burial.

Embolism An embolus is usually a piece of clot that has broken away from a thrombus. It can also be formed from clumps of bacteria, fat globules, or even air bubbles. Origi-nating in a blood vessel, it travels until it wedges in a narrowing blood vessel, preventing blood circulation. In the

arteries to the brain it can be responsi-ble for a STROKE or CVA.
SEE ALSO: THROMBOSIS

Embryo In higher plants and most animals the growing fertilized egg is called an embryo. A human offspring is called an embryo during the first two months of pregnancy and a FETUS after that time.

Embryology   (em-bree-AHL-uh-jee) Many animals begin life as a fertilized egg. Each one grows into the form of an adult animal—for example, a frog, a chicken, or a man. The study of the changes that take place as an egg de-velops into a fully-developed animal is the science of embryology.

From earliest times, men have shown a great interest in the way that animals come into being. ARISTOTLE, a Greek of ancient times, described the changes he saw as a chick developed within the egg. During the Dark Ages, most people did not question the origin of life. With the rebirth of free thinking during the RENAISSANCE (around 1500 A.D.), the question of how ani-mals form arose once again. It was assumed that the adult animal was present in the egg in miniature form. According to this idea, development proceeded by the gradual unfolding and enlargement of the tiny parts. This was called the *preformation theory*. Until this theory was proved false, no science of embryology was possible.

Wolff (1733–1794) was the first to argue that the embryo begins as a uniform mass of material within the egg. He thought that the mass gradually became organized into more and more complex structures. This theory was called *epigenesis*. It is the foun-dation of modern embryology. VON BAER (1792–1876) discovered the egg of the

DEVELOPMENT OF THE CHICK

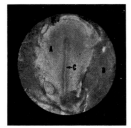

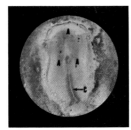

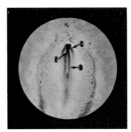

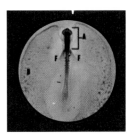

13-hour chick embryo: A—inner part of embryo; B—blood cells forming; C—primitive streak, where main body forms

Brain region (within the A's) is starting to form in 18-hour embryo. The streak at C is a little thicker

In 21-hour chick, folded streak at C will form brain. At E, ridges will form tube. Lumps at D will be muscles

28-hour chick: A—brain; F—large veins; B—blood islands are growing together to form blood vessels

Photo-micrographs by National Teaching Aids, Inc.

The heart (H) of a 38-hour chick has started beating. The brain at A has developed five distinct regions

The 48-hour chick embryo has started to bend in the head area and also twist onto the side

In the 56-hour chick, the head is almost developed: H—heart; G—eye; J—ear; F—large arteries forming

96-hour chick: G—eye; K—front limb buds; L—back limb buds; M—sac that receives wastes from the embryo

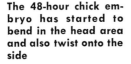

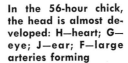

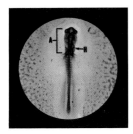

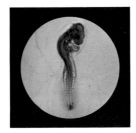

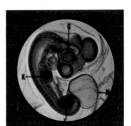

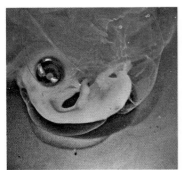

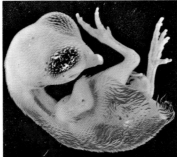

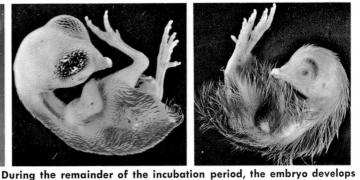

During the remainder of the incubation period, the embryo develops into a complete chick: (above, left to right)—8th day, 12th day, 14th day. After hatching at 21 days, the feather covering changes as the down is replaced by pin feathers: (below, left to right)—2nd day after hatching, 12th day, 19th day

Florence Stuck

mammal which develops inside the animal. He also set forth the theory of germ layers.

After 1839, when Schleiden and SCHWANN presented the theory that the cell is the unit of organization of living forms, embryonic development was recognized as a continuous process of cell division and cell specialization.

Embryology has passed through three stages. First, the events of development were carefully *described*. Then, types of embryonic development in different animals were *compared*. Balfour (1851–1882) was a leader in the field of comparative embryology. The field of embryology today is an *experimental* science. Embryologists devise experiments to discover how the processes of development occur, and what principles will explain them. Driesch, Roux, Spemann, Harrison, and Holtfreter are important pioneers of experimental embryology.

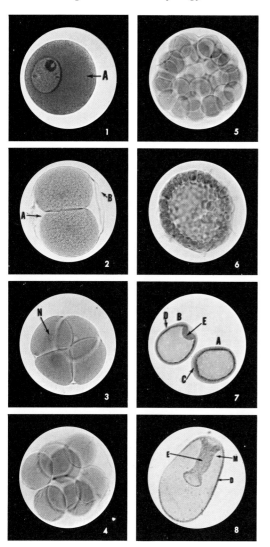

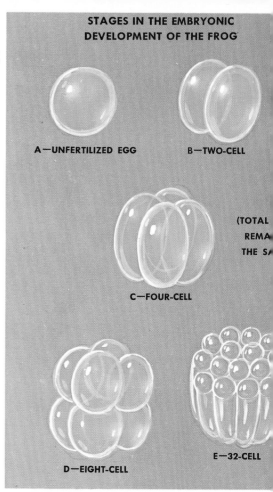

STAGES IN THE EMBRYONIC
DEVELOPMENT OF THE FROG

A—UNFERTILIZED EGG   B—TWO-CELL

(TOTAL
REMA
THE SA

C—FOUR-CELL

D—EIGHT-CELL   E—32-CELL

The illustrations at the left show cleavage in the egg cells of a starfish. Its early stages of development are similar to those of man and other animals. Shortly afterward, they assume the form of the developing starfish and become very different.

(1) Fertilized egg—zygote; (2) first cleavage—two cells; (3) second cleavage—four cells; (4) third cleavage—eight cells; (5) a later stage—a mass of cells; (6) blastula—the hollow ball of cells; (7) two embryos in the early gastrula stage; (8) late gastrula stage

Photo-micrographs by National Teaching Aids, Inc.

STAGES OF DEVELOPMENT
IN VERTEBRATES

1. *Fertilization:* The first cell of each new animal is the fertilized egg. It is called a *zygote*. This one-celled zygote is formed by the union of two cells called *gametes*. The male sperm and the female egg are both gametes. The genes inside the gametes control the pattern of development and the characteristics of the new animal. The environment that the developing egg is in also affects the pattern of development.

2. *Cleavage:* After fertilization, the parts of the egg are reorganized. Cell division then begins. The zygote divides into two cells,

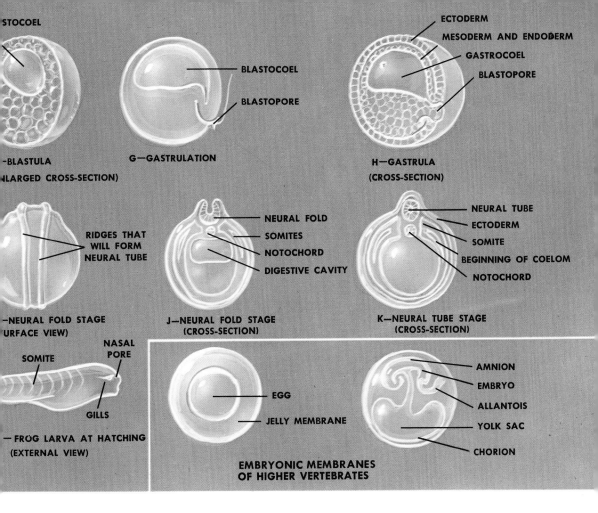

STOCOEL

BLASTOCOEL

BLASTOPORE

-BLASTULA
NLARGED CROSS-SECTION)

G—GASTRULATION

ECTODERM

MESODERM AND ENDODERM

GASTROCOEL

BLASTOPORE

H—GASTRULA
(CROSS-SECTION)

RIDGES THAT
WILL FORM
NEURAL TUBE

-NEURAL FOLD STAGE
URFACE VIEW)

NEURAL FOLD
SOMITES
NOTOCHORD
DIGESTIVE CAVITY

J—NEURAL FOLD STAGE
(CROSS-SECTION)

NEURAL TUBE
ECTODERM
SOMITE
BEGINNING OF COELOM
NOTOCHORD

K—NEURAL TUBE STAGE
(CROSS-SECTION)

NASAL
PORE
SOMITE

GILLS

—FROG LARVA AT HATCHING
(EXTERNAL VIEW)

EGG

JELLY MEMBRANE

AMNION
EMBRYO
ALLANTOIS
YOLK SAC
CHORION

EMBRYONIC MEMBRANES
OF HIGHER VERTEBRATES

then into four, then into eight, and so on—until hundreds of cells are formed. These cell divisions occur in regular patterns, depending on the type of animal developing. For example, the cell divisions of a chicken are different from the cell divisions of a frog. The difference in cell divisions creates the final difference in animals. The cell divisions are called CLEAVAGE patterns.

3. *Blastula:* When a hollow ball of many cells has been formed, the embryo is called a *blastula.* The blastula has a single layer of cells. The space within the blastula is the *blastocoel.*

4. *Gastrula:* Two layers of cells are then formed from the blastula by the process of *gastrulation.* This process begins in a certain region of the blastula called the *blastopore,* where cells turn inward and move to form an inner layer of cells next to the outer layer. A new space is formed, called the *gastrocoel.* This space is the primitive or early form of the digestive cavity. This two-layered stage is the gastrula.

5. *Germ layers:* The germ layers are the original cells that produce the later organs of the animal. The outer tissue layer is the *ectoderm.* It will form the epidermis of the skin, the NERVOUS SYSTEM, and the sense organs, such as the eye and ear. The inner tissue layer lining the gastrocoel is the *endoderm.* It will form the digestive tract, including the glands that aid digestion, such as the pancreas and the liver. The RESPIRATORY SYSTEM is also formed from the endoderm. A third layer of cells, called the *mesoderm,* grows out of the inner lining of the gastrula. The mesoderm will form the noto chord, the skeleton, the muscles, the heart, the blood vessels, the connective tissues, the kidneys, and the reproductive organs.

6. *The neural tube:* In the middle back area of the embryo, a narrow strip of mesodermal cells become specialized into an organ called the *notochord.* This serves as a stiffening rod of support when its cells become filled with a thick jelly-like substance. In early stages of the embryo, the notochord is very important in organizing the development of the nervous system. The ectoderm that lies directly above the notochord will develop into the nervous system. All other

✳ THINGS TO DO

WATCHING THE CHANGES IN THE DEVELOPMENT OF A CHICK EMBRYO

1. Place two dozen fertile chicken eggs in a commercial incubator or a home-made one (see **INCUBATOR** for directions).
2. Secure a bottle of rubbing alcohol or dilute formaldehyde solution to be used as a preservative for the chick embryos.
3. Starting on the third day of incubation, break open an egg each day. Carefully remove the embryo and put it in a bottle of preservative.
4. Continue the procedure for eighteen days. Observe the changes that occur in the embryonic development from egg to chick.

ectoderm will become skin tissue. The nervous system begins as a plate of specialized cells which thicken to form two long ridges. These ridges eventually meet and close over to form the hollow neural tube. The ectodermal skin grows over the surface of the neural tube, covering it. The forward part of the neural tube will become the brain, while the posterior part will develop into the spinal cord.

7. *The mesoderm:* The mesoderm forms, in addition to the notochord, blocks of tissue on each side of the notochord. These segment blocks, called *somites,* will form the dermis of the skin, the vertebrae of the backbone, and the muscles of the trunk. Loose cells, called the *mesenchyme* cells, wander out from the mesoderm to form tissues of other parts of the body. The mesoderm also sends out two layers of cells which form a lining of the coelom, or body cavity. The kidney and reproductive organs are formed from this lining.

EMBRYONIC MEMBRANES

As the young embryo develops, it has very little power to protect itself from the hardships of the world around it. The parents often succeed in giving protection to their young. In the case of the frog, eggs are laid in large clusters and are protected by jelly membranes which keep them afloat. These membranes surround the embryos until they hatch as larvae. Larvae are free-living animals that are not yet fully mature. They find their own food. Later the tadpole LARVA changes into an adult frog and is able to live on land.

Birds and reptiles do not usually live in water and must find a different way to protect their young. The fertilized eggs, laid on land, are surrounded by a hard but porous shell. Inside the shell the embryo develops in a sac of fluid. The *amnion,* as this sac is called, protects the embryo from jarring shocks and from drying out. There are also other embryonic membranes that make it possible for the embryo to stay alive. The *yolk sac* connects with the digestive tract and contains a large store of food which feeds the embryo as it develops. The *allantois* is another membrane which connects with the digestive tract, but at its posterior end. The allantois is not only an exit for wastes formed by the embryo as it grows, but it is also very important as a respiratory sac. Exchange of gases occurs between the

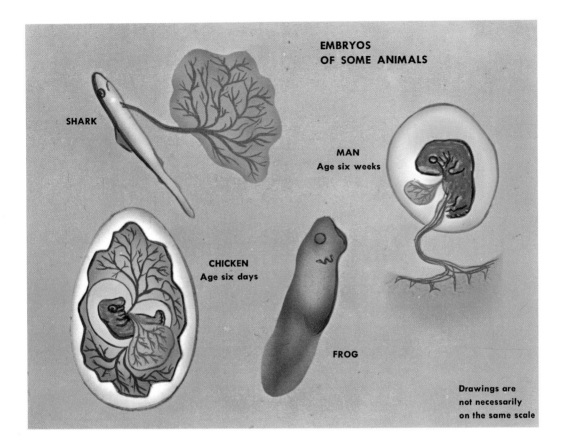

EMBRYOS
OF SOME ANIMALS

SHARK

MAN
Age six weeks

CHICKEN
Age six days

FROG

Drawings are
not necessarily
on the same scale

membrane and the outside air through the porous shell. Part of the allantois remains in the adult animal as the urinary bladder. All the membranes are generously supplied with blood vessels leading into the embryo.

In mammals, a great advance has been made in protecting the developing embryo. The fertilized egg is not laid outside the body of the mother, but instead develops inside its body. The egg is fertilized in the oviduct of the mother and begins its early development there. By the time the embryo is in the blastula stage it has traveled into the uterus, where it burrows into the lining of this organ. A new organ, called the *placenta,* forms. This brings the blood vessels of the mother into close relation with the blood vessels of the embryo. Food and oxygen pass through the blood vessel walls of the mother into the blood vessels of the embryo. Carbon dioxide and other wastes from the embryo also pass across into the blood vessels of the mother to be carried away. However, the blood of the mother and the embryo never mix directly with one another.

Because the mother supplies the embryo with food, no yolk is necessary in the egg of the mammal, and none is present. An amnion surrounds the mammalian embryo in a fluid bath. A *chorion,* which is a union of membranes that are originally part of the amnion and allantois, forms the embryonic part of the placenta.

The embryo develops well protected in the uterus through the time called the GESTATION PERIOD. This time varies among mammals. In the mouse it is 21 days. In man it is nine months. In the elephant it is 21 months. At the end of gestation, the uterus contracts and expels the developed embryo, or fetus, into the outside world, and the birth of the new individual occurs. The newly born mammal is still not fully developed and still must undergo many changes in growth. The parent continues to protect its young until it is mature—first, by providing milk for its food; then, by teaching it to live in the environment to which it must adjust.   B. B. G.

SEE ALSO: ANATOMY; ANIMALS, CLASSIFICATION OF; BIOGENETIC LAW; CELLS; CIRCULATORY SYSTEM; MAMMALIA; REPRODUCTION, ASEXUAL; REPRODUCTIVE SYSTEMS

Conversion Factors
to Metric Measurement

Length
1 inch = 25.4 millimeters (mm) exactly
1 inch = 2.54 centimeters (cm) exactly
1 foot = 0.3048 meters (m) exactly
1 yard = 0.9144 meters (m) exactly
1 mile = 1.609344 kilometers (km) exactly

Area
1 square inch = 6.4516 square centimeters (cm^2) exactly
1 square foot = 0.092903 square meters (m^2)
1 square yard = 0.836127 square meters (m^2)
1 square acre = 0.404686 hectares (ha)
1 square mile = 2.58999 square kilometers (km^2)

Cubic Measure
1 cubic inch = 16.387064 cubic centimeters (cm^3) exactly
1 cubic foot = 0.0283168 cubic meters (m^3)
1 cubic yard = 0.764555 cubic meters (m^3)

US Liquid Measure
1 fluid ounce = 29.5735 milliliters (ml)
1 fluid ounce = 0.2957 deciliters (dl)
1 pint = 0.473176 liters (l)
1 gallon = 3.78541 liters (l)

US Dry Measure
1 pint = 0.550610 liters (l)
1 bushel = 35.2391 liters (l)

Weight
1 grain = 0.0647989 grams (g)
1 ounce = 28.3495 grams (g)
1 pound = 0.453592 kilograms (kg)
1 short ton = 0.907185 metric tons (t)
1 UK ton = 1.01605 metric tons (t)

Temperature
To convert Fahrenheit to Centigrade (Celsius) complete the following
equation. $(F° - 32) \times 5 \div 9 = C°$